The City Keeps

John Godfrey

Wave Books Seattle and New York

The City Keeps

Selected and New Poems 1966–2014

Published by Wave Books

www.wavepoetry.com

Wave Books titles are distributed to the trade by

Consortium Book Sales and Distribution

Phone: 800-283-3572 / SAN 631-760X

Library of Congress Cataloging-in-Publication Data

Godfrey, John, 1945–

[Poems. Selections]

The city keeps : selected and new poems 1966–2014 /

John Godfrey. — First edition.

pages ; cm

ISBN 978-1-940696-26-3 (limited edition hardcover)

ISBN 978-1-940696-31-7 (softcover)

I. Title.

PS3557.O29A6 2016

811'.54—dc23

2015026557

"Trip Wire" was published in *The Chicago Review*, issue 58:3/4.

"Evidence" and "One Hand" were published in *Sal Mimeo 10*.

The author is grateful to the Z Foundation for a fellowship that enabled
the making of this book. Thanks to Larry Fagin for editorial consultation.
Thanks to Miles Champion for digitalizing pre-digital texts.

Designed and composed by Quemadura

Printed in the United States of America

9 8 7 6 5 4 3 2 1

First Edition

from Dabble [1982]

from **Where the Weather Suits My Clothes** [1984]

from **Midnight on Your Left** [1988]

from **Push the Mule** [2001]

from **Private Lemonade** [2003]

from City of Corners [2008]

from **Singles and Fives** [2011]

from **Tiny Gold Dress** [2012]

from Gold Stars Wet Hearts [2014]

from **Knee-length Black** [2014]

Uncollected Poems [2011–2014]

Dedicated to those who people the City of New York

from

26 Poems

(Adventures in Poetry, 1971)

Touch

The gauntlet puts on weight
and I climb into its thumb

which balances and then teeters
and thuds against my nose

and I see stars forever having
forgot aspirations of diligence and method

whatever was the retreat in research
and pursuit in gravity of something

to do while resting in geological sleep
where to touch is to be felt by nothing

Sonnet

Harbor open your eyes
Mermaids chatter under a mango tree
and on a bridge a captain spills the beans
They collect in a hat immeasurable
and the dipstick disappears like a
sinking book when patriotic sex goes
by collecting for the March of Dimes
That will cost you a pretty penny
On its face is a profile entombed
in the heart and soul of the inventor
of the Planetary Transmission
Put the lever in the first position
and engage the Trois Morceaux
Dizzy Dean, Amos 'n' Andy, René Magritte

Poem

The gravity of our situation is matched
Only by my desire for a tremendous electrical storm.
You will take this to heart, I am sure,
And claim that it is also your desire.
Meanwhile, I feel that I may never talk much
In the desolation of a "medium setting."
That is to say, to be a stranger and alone there
Does not insure a distinct appraisal of you where you always were.
But none of this is new to you, and you have many assets
That will assure you of years of recognition
In just those yards where holidays are determined.
You will soon notice the effects of not missing you at all
Wafted in the gentle manner of a code
Condensed from a fragment of greetings.

Sonnet

Eyes to no awesome wind, bred
white with the slim repose of the thief,
we nose out into the pillow that surrounds
the waste of all the world from us, and for
a moment no chance knows the peace
of a passed chance, no thief could avoid
despair on the balcony, where his hands
turn into the spoils he has imagined.

There are words for a deception that passes
observation as sound passes the ear, oblivious.
There are men who hate and know only fruition
from a plateau that prohibits perspective.
The sea might turn into sky, the birds to
stars, your breath bring gold to life.

Rain Waste

I am tired of blooey and fud.
Tell me, do the long arms of the dark woman
still reach down through the rainy clouds
and move me on like a bale of cotton?

In the rain is a lotion that has caused kings to die
and lesser men to stand cross-eyed in a pelting rain.
But tear up your map of Europe; put your exotic
currencies behind you: you are saturated with their

petty embargoes, like the captain of the ship, who,
once put out to a long dangerous cruise, decides
who should work and how hard. He knows his tyranny.
His excesses reflect upon the Europe he has left behind.

A tiny star tumbles into infinity.
Many men will immediately race after it.
In the vacuum they leave behind, my laziness will expand
and become the world's most prominent fixture.

First Taste

It enters my ears: snow
and outside willy-nilly inside
known as passion, faces gone
where glasses rest to correct 20/20 vision
The Good Companion of the Imperial Sepulchre
bathing scaled creatures in glassine fluid
and, in turn, they speak for themselves.
It is easy to turn a face towards you
walking in wet heavy snow
                          in high and dry love
cagey with your substance that is subject
to concentrations of blood and anonymous palms
slick with intentions. Intentions are realized,
I admit, in the most humble of seasons, winter,
or maybe in the first taste of a season,
winter, or in the changing tastes of any season,
winter. It is baffling to feel sweet under
the ideal strivings. And it is intimate to
be baffled by you, and it is none too soon for me.
For me all snow collects in your hair.
Where snow accumulates, men can play as
youth does, in season, and hard lessons
ride out to sea, first by bird, and then
by reason.
          By reason men know what they are,

and then they turn back to the vagueness of
the cache of quick feelings, less and less
predominate. I gather together the warmest
matter I know, and out through melting snow
to hear you, as crows fly, as wires sustain
them.

Month

The giant woman fondles my breast.
I am crashing through my visit
Like a broad red stain. The carpeting
Launches help from the mountains,
Notes are straining like tubas for
The highest place, each excitedly isolated
From prospects of entering life and falling.
Interest in the envelope is flagging;
The arms are dirty to the elbow
In the torso of this solid month.

The Works

With all the flowering crispness of daylight
in Singapore, four spare hours are set aside
like abandoned hockey skates. And to the trained
eye, they are not puffed-up sensibilities
barnstorming through the terrestrial backfield
with not a ball but a pillow, poised toward
             one of a myriad of other
             places to be. It is elixir
             substantive
   and it is time we appraised
   the sullen and unpredictable
   less worthy for slaying half-night's
   obstinacy, and the summer more
   unanswerable for guarding us with
   gods,
             ripped with its own suffusion
             of a woman lying in the sun
             overhung with trees

Little Sister

Some funky bullshit, and hard by
Did that nasty old car run you over?
On the mercantile street an occasional
               sleek one with
               a cherry cone
holds a light for you in her cupped hands
and tells you the nonsense that began in New York
that day you took her down the street and bought
her a shoeshine   Aquiline
Thank you, I already have a heroic Vietnamese woman
Hands shaping the clouds to day in the North
feed pussy
have fun
out of the shade and laurels

Our Knees

I would like a word with you
now that the night is through
              with you
       and your faculty of making
even the most awful burden seem wild
and its wind seem grand in your hearing.
      The flag of my ship rolls
    in the darkness and the helm
      turns cold under your gaze.
Is it your manner that dissolves the darkness
or is it my unsteadiness that
makes the room possible where trumpets
ordain our togetherness?
         These are the properties of a rash dream
that we, upon waking, haul ourselves
out of bed and to our knees
to guess at its origins and what
its place is in our lives
     or we fasten our boots
       through the blast of smoke
        that surrounds us like a king.

Poem

At home in the diner, flagman sprints
past adrape with flags, we have been
promised glory but instead twin arms
descend from the skies to smother us with puppy love.
                        It's really okay.
            I got this mountain that way.
                                Here, let me throw this switch
        for you
and the flames will reach up to lick
the heels of a baby with the face
of the earth.

from

3 Poems

(Bouwerie Editions, 1973)

Love Knife

My true friends will slop gin on my fresh grave
but now I would like to tell you of the beauty of your thighs
to which I press my lips without a word
There is fog outside it screens us into three other worlds
and we who love sundown will know it's there, runway
as it adds a flutter to our appetites a bow-wow
that without being triggered is just an ordinary bomb
Our mulish although picturesque neighborhood hangs out
dressed flashy but cheap in its doorways and beatup cars
but I was born to populate a continent singlehanded!
Space and time and general human gotcha
have confounded me and left me all these pleasures instead
The pleasure of escape the pleasure of refusal
the pleasure of abandon the pleasure of renewal
the pleasure of having nothing against being in your arms
the pleasure of an old-fashioned vision of Venus
who screams plump and billowy against an eternal sky
blue and cloudless tipping out of her seashell
which is the measure of the jealousy you cause her
when your hand instructs the lightning to start my heart

Radiant Dog

Radiant dog on doublecross, and I,
by night, a raven fly. My fear
is that eternity has an alm
that is ordinary to ten thousand
and worn from my strings, my console
of limbs, and I a missing part.
It is the world that's new, not I,
and submarines can shoot the land
from the wheelbarrow of sickly pastorals.
Give me the swamp any day! or the huts
that pave the slave to freedom.
From a small cloud in my ears
the song has leapt the valley
curtained with snow, and for ascendant
harmony the gambler thumbs his cards.
Of all the queens one is a witch
whose curse is that she's held.
The horses roll the stone and trot
after their maturity sweepstakes.
This time the homeliest won't ride
my bet into hasty subtract glue.
The pieces fly and here I lie,
triangle of head and gut and thigh.
Put me on my mount, Tomahawk, and

past the river our cortege will dust
the heavy fur, and peasants' prayers
will touch the smell of holy cadaver.
I will have sun and manly rage,
and Mike Atlas will trim me up
to rip the bier from my brother's
hearse, and avenge me for my loss.
The gallows hurt! and for my scheme
I hang on the bridge's span
where my mother will trust my lips
with tears, the ones I send her now.

Gray Blazing Pit

A short bright street, a brighter park at its end
The dissipated jewels of winter ping my face and hands
    which are warmer than the ragged desperation of a cold
    heavy habit harboring the body of a junkie street
    marshal, and, no, he is not as bright
    as this day, the changing of warm air cells
The cough and orange, lime, and mocha churn from door to door
    and, reminded of the dowry she fears
    an old lady leaves her window
    over the avenue to take a painful piss
Poor men are taking their wives to hospitals, lunar orphans
    run in school corridors, ship blast from river
    echoes, and young energy up to no good finds me
    no earthly paradise wherein to trampoline
A young girl whose body is beginning to round daydreams
    is troubled and senses things that speed
    as if her face were bathed in tears knowing already
    she will exhaust onrushing longing
Her and her boy of an old man bestowing her cherry
    upon hostile memory, her distress and pain, his
    unmindful ineptness, sullen humiliated braggadocio
Someone now is being slain, the Tombs seethes and trembles
    here, one of the dark places of the earth, shines before
    its children raid its afternoon and evening

But a Diane sings over a casserole, one strung-out Carl smiles
        leadenly warming hands at a laundry's vent
O for a thin wrist rouged with love in which my stain may culture!
        is the poem of streetlamp
All too weakly I think of you, an adorable sorcerer, *lumière*
These irreparable gnaws, is there gauze for this ecstasy?
The gentle sea is for theaters, and vertigos of activity
        slip us our bonanza on slimy silver
My image, one and only, corrects brother shades
        an understanding about them with the sun
That charmed dollar bills fill my stash and berries
        ripen in cellar gardens under two dreaming women
        who make love to each other
That erotic medals set in rings tell fortunes in song
That spurned orchestras are powerful gods whom it is natural
        to worship floating free on atoms of drink
        jamming through kettles of perfected decay
Then freedom will become the soul and mansions host untroubled
        laboratories of beauty where all flaws certainly
        wave their own insigned vests, arms swinging
        a parade distributed by centimeters between red and violet
The marchers occupy the rainbow's end of constant nativity
        bearing ironic palm branches in celebration
The child will not be assassinated even though
        he comprehends error
        and is inspired by strangulation
        and the virginity of attention both

Who will pole his punt down a Hudson in the Sun, defining
    a composite fleece from the millions of down that will have
    brushed on arching waists beside him in alert passions
And doom not sacrifice calisthenic impulse under awnings of slavery
    nor we retch on cotton spaghetti of enervated reach
But drifting boat dwellers will power the Sun with their concise
    melodies in which a tension conducts the light of dreams
    to embody the invisible woman awaking in want again

from

Music of
the Curbs

(Adventures in Poetry, 1976)

Equinox

The confidence and purity
of afternoon light
come as a stranger
nude among apples!
With coffee, 35¢
But I am not moving today
among aimless phantasmal
peccaries, jungles of
soothing exertions
I am not mothering
myself into knots
on stakes heathens
measure with their eyes
over arrows
        But the avenue's
chant blows cold
        over the sensuous wide-faced sea
over the sensual cling of pants
        felt through gloves
for hunger communicates in a darkness
        phosphorescently negative
and as hot as bright, behind the eyes
        where the growing sun is a humor

Atlas

Ribbon of municipal trees, weary with molecules of
strain, velvet teeth that might as well
be coming down on me while I'm off-poise
on my marsupial feet, a wombat in love with
an infinity around which he can build nothing.

Well, I'm weary too. I've been swamped with
gutters and my hands are not the color of my face.
There are too many voices in out of the sun,
where there should be smoldering stumps.

Purple journey in a comic Ford,
understand me, my little red lines
that give you an idea of clouds of dust
under landings where you lose your shoes.

The Music of the Curbs

The note that is played only by angels
kicks dirt in my face and strings red lights
to brassiere the soft, smooth matrons who
sit in my lap blowing smoke in my ear
They leave when my teeth fall out and the patch
drops from an empty eye into my clumsy grog
But it is summer, for laughs I go around feeling too much
Gallantry causes me to be better strong than smart
and the pungent compress falls like the bugle
of a ransomer in the hayloft of my heart, flurry
of skirts, sinking back into the trapdoor of fear
The puke-faced beggar-lady in overcoats
trailing her satchels of cans, bottles, papers, and twine
asks me why, if I am not an aesthete, I am not a believer
and something turns over, the drama in his pajamas
that splits open the head of America's chaplain, Melville
Granted we must have our mythical sailors of unprincipled
awakeness to challenge catastrophes of air into breath
but years spent trying to realize an idea are hurdled
or dead birds drinking at tribal gutters, the same thing
Both ways the liver goes, the heart's a wreck, blood green,
etc., and suddenly, holding others off, looking left
and downwards, I am god—reading the *Swiss-Up Gazette*!

Morning Star

Morning star of leaves, long blue arm of alcohol
and, around my waist, sleep, like a grin, bowing along
lifeless streets where bundles of *The News* drop
unreadably in the radiant gray to the east
that improves, swallowed by red, orange, then yellow
No words, no auxiliary pronunciation except for heat
renewed from where it never slept, mourned

I unlock and empty the cellos I see, and, like the apostle
of chance, I disintegrate, a word that has collided
with the high, broad forehead of a beautiful woman
and, indecipherable, is right now flowing over her lips

The one for whom love would never dispel isolation
longs not to have loved evil for nothing, *jeux de cartes*
and deletes the natural death of a glorious impracticality

like morning's, the death of a winter that leaves me very sad
rebounding from the luxuriant, overconfident surrender
that made me dizzy with sun and amused
at my reflection in bragging thieves and cowed
daybreak bells of St. Brigid's terrorized by sunset

There were pampered tropical birds, and rafts of clowns
on the river, and the bridge a pinwheel of tension
Well, the clowns were the last to be wrecked by vanishing waves
and enchantment leaves the child who begins a sad anger
because he is interested in life and steals cars

Come April

While the air is soft, before the thunder
fourth graders with tattered notebooks haunt
the cuchifritos and their older brothers plague
a few stairwells crossing town to Nathan's
Eggplant bristles in sidewalk boxes on Avenue C
adjacent a larval well formed by an empty treebed
A smile in street cats' eyes could be any kind of dope
Voices universally spit out shrill colloquial jive
Regardless of her husky mastiff, Amos Rico asks
a young blonde in maxi passing the laundromat
if he might plunge his tongue in her timid chasm—
she doesn't answer, hardly looks, and her Fido
drops an enormous, awesomely firm turd at the crosswalk
The widow of an old pensioner passes at a shuffle
carefully steering her almost-empty shopping cart
She looks distrustfully at someone
and tells herself "Everything's wrong!"
But the three schoolgirls on this busy sidewalk
are still enchanted, with each other's dark prettiness
and the filth and cobbled avenue are for *los otros*

These streets are like clouds in the valley where I am giant
And I am not stoned-out in a silver garbage can about to
attempt the falls surrounding Ponce or Candelabra!

Let me be overpowered by lecherous spring, as the busdriver
is, holding the door open an extra few moments, the more to
gander at two long, slim brown legs in candyapple hotpants!
Naked to the toes, let me sweat the days longer, pausing
with aching tongue and dong in the unmistakable!
Bump Lulu in her toggle, peck a groove, squander tadpoles
bounce laughing down stoops of box springs, forget that
King Kong love will spoil, except for crazy slaves
except for juicy handicraft, clown to dawn!

Idiots

There is a dry breeze, the moon is surrounded
by haze, the shelters cave in and drear elation
sponges through hazards that remain unknown
tonight, where women and men establish
a flesh in air, groping on steeples, tossing
in cars, remote in diners, rowdy on stoops
Some are sober-faced, powdered, and strutting
notoriously, others cautiously still their hands
These are not years when many are noisy for long
Crude though, and hideous, mean, inescapable, vindictive
Empty conquest pastilles crown their sprues of dream
Nobody needs his fortune told anymore under wailing domes
as an original young man dies on the toilet having
transformed metropolis into a giant booby trap for balloons
And now it is my task to transform chromium to an embrace
anticipated by the heart, which stings in defeat, rocking
its history in spumes of cum and patrolling onyx flash
But the troops are lushed on marquees sponsored by women
who breathe satisfaction and loathe the hunchback
who has torn down the banners they had strung
across streets—a hail of bullets tears his head!
But they are easily forgotten, who needs eyes!
Who needs shoulders if angels are unable to survive!

Who needs the intelligence of nerve most cruel to total love!
which is over, says the rotting pigeon with a franc in its beak
and the pure idiots are volunteered to be punished
by an understanding which unleashes their appetites

Love Peon

Kings embalmed with saffron, obese angels rising
from the park trickling dogs, young black man with
creased fists and a terrible look of sour immediacy—

All I have to tell is of longing, of my demented and desperate
heart which billiards off the woman who brushes
roaches with wings from my chest and confuses

hard truth in the air of dingy waste and discontent
with the roar and despairing hiss beyond which
she is magnificent and the last animal kisses her knee!

I would be a speck on her tongue, an invisible moistness
high on her thigh, a charged humidity of fur!
I would disappear for her, I would murder her and

carry her stiff on my shoulder through flaming tenements!
We must touch nipples and fold our hairs together
and the twisted coathangers in my chest will strengthen

rather than drill my heart—I come into my hand
and pour it into my mouth, which I imagine is hers!
When will I be pacified by her gentle intelligence, when

will the pain of longing for her passionate expertise be
soothed and the dwarf who weeps in garbage be consoled?
I am nothing, no hopes, no yearning to dump sand

into toy scrimmages camping on simpleminded love!
Let me see her hand beside her face and suck on her ear!
Have her pour her jarring tamarindos through my nostrils!

I will forget slings and syringes, warrior lice of fear!
Will she forget me again and shine my dereliction?
O let me kick her! Let me handle her with my legs!

Where are the four thousand Turks that are holding her
imprisoned in cold flat mosaic and silence?
I'll slash and bleed my way to her body and die!

La Gloire

I want it to be allowed to happen for
what it is, how it is done: without waste,
which it is very like. Take "Grooveyard"
by Monk; the smoothness is a complexity
become manageable, such as the theft of a saddle
from an arsonist performing rider, stationed
at the Circus, to be plucked like
a sty from under a lavender lid by the
grave roundness of a moon, bloodletting magnet
The heart reeks with the knowledge of
stupidity, to the exclusion of lust, the humming
Or is that a transvestite Br'er Fudge
hooching in the lingerie I hear, a global blow?
If in this world, whose career is to change
beliefs in life, I am to accept the human
as master, my character alone will decide
my destructions and fruitions, converging
sacraments I see them as, as water loves air,
as neckties love laughter, as prisoners love money
And desires—kisses, moistures—that fleshly
awake with the sun that is almost too honest

Saint Augustine

Snow, like albino hornets
flurries through the bars
half gray, half silver
in death row's daylight
The silence is studied:
breathing can be heard
but the man remains un-
defined, a shadow erected
in bright yellow light
around the corner's fence
He is relishing a dream
of Renaissance squalor
where the music is of reeds
bridging mountains' winds
across the hot springs nearby
the castle's foot where he
stands immersed in thought
of himself, in order to
account for his presence
and the sex of his banner

Peaches

There's no reason but luck, she's
Queen of the Hydrant, Peaches
      the same eight years old
      as the hit single
      that inspired her name
I mean, her mama wants her pretty
not just clean, hair straightened
      rolled into a droplet
      over her right ear
      with that Sudanese
      Sheen of the Ancients
      black glass for iris
self-assurance and benignity
of the very-well-loved
and joyous teeth of
welcoming expression, gracefully
unselfconscious of her seductive
tail, angel web from pinkies
      It works, she is encircled
      by the children who love
      more than envy her
before whom the prettiest Ukrainian princess
granted thoughtless hugs, exchanges
intimacies of the latent years with
the purest holy lesserness

from

Dabble

(Full Court Press, 1982)

Schnapps Sonata

When filled with, say, flakes
air softens the senses
In pointillistic smokiness
they are dismantling the stage
and removing the chairs
of history, and I attach
effortlessly to the slippery promenades
someone between thief and medic
A calm grown giant, like an aspirin
gongs inside me, assenting to
every inflamed word posted
through naked gods, delusions
or the commodious ring of truth
I'm in no position to quibble
the hasty nightfall is issuing
its demands for signification
that are only fulfilled unconsciously
like forgetting, but never the ear
The ear is hungry, it drapes
like a nightgown over
a keyboard, it hasn't softened
the ear is a classical man

Dabble

Dabble hours heave all muggy
with Miss Subway's sighs
In a mood like California crime
my tippling love swells nightly
in tempo abreast liberating nuisance
Scat-voiced bouquets tendered
your maternal side by
the infantile mob, and you
return a kiss, its tactile oval nudge
blown as casually as a hit
of reefer toward their reddened eyes
and myths of doe-like women—
squandered musky intent, eh legs?—
falling from sprouted whole-grain skies
Not a bedroom scene, more as if
on a fender, surrounded by the affronting
petals of dog where the *barranca* curb
hands to the river draught
the lilies of storm drains
We overlook this, but not the
vaudevillian *angst* of strays courting
invulnerable windows, parroting
sleepers' far-gone postures with
savant economy, the purest jazz

Mirrors at Night

Downpour rounding up
the lively West sidewalks
and paroling faces to
fast-food corners, nickel 'n' dime
It's relaxing to throw
the declining speedball
pearl before a barbecue pork
and onions at midnight
among self-possessed every-
day dudes who cause a lot
of excitement, out
of a shockingly bland
wisdom that would have
long ago convinced me
that loneliness and blackness
are my greatest confusion

Loneliness after all
loneliness is the part
of the animal that is
too civilized, appearances
aside, for generously
gratuitous intimacies, out
of vanity, of course, arrogance

and the uncertain benevolence
that discovers in the
blackness the ambitious models
for my unwilling aboriginal
fear, my self-hate
adept and precise, pairing
off lusts and intuitions
developing fictions that
include sinks and menstruation
and I evade the river pygmies
thoroughly enervated by
the remote baleful womanliness
of my bedraggled companion
who wears injuries like furs

Poem

Mezzanines of nightfall clashing like
the blue of your shirt with the blue
of her eyes, who stalls gusts with
foam and wreathing, harbinger saxophones
immense in pride—so Autumn's rule
sheathed despite wrinkles in woolen
dances, never forsakes its hurricane
It feels indispensable, which is quite
all right during a tide without lights
dreaming of alternate preoccupations
your greater richness, courage, or
mastery would confide to you, by you, there
But you are overgenerous, you are
equally awake when light reappears
when a simple steampipe becomes Ionic
and you once again abhor murder, pledge love

By Antique Vogues

Dun, dun, dun, more dun
Ah! that's truly a mauve
Now the clouddom is more
real because more sophisticated
in lieu of life, of extract

Even the evictees, selling
belongings on the sidewalk
to get together their pints
express a sophistication in
their irrepressible dance of loss
I remember their attitude
in an impersonal vastness
of memory, as if I stood
alone in a renaissance city
and it were a useless aptitude
of the view, to be so solitary

Unholy Spring

Insomniac trees rattle silken little
tongues, emphasis all day-bleached
and charm accompanies vigilance
past fenced park gates for
a circular stroll among *el pueblo bajo*
Your shirt, amigo, should be salmon
and your mustache nurse birdlings
but I am sure you are fruitful
in some other meager way you daily forget
Balm is the blue sleeve returned
to the sky, and brown people
baring their arms, such candy!
And so much impatience, beneath
char tones of premature boughs
as the spirit climbs, fingers
threatened by boots, and desperate
I walk brittle grass well armed
unweighed by hopeful goblets
My profile conveyed in dust afresh
concedes nothing, as it and light enmesh

Double Sonnet

The rain, confined to dignity
does not dizzy the trees
and the breath-like smell of thought
lays against the brick walls
as so much yellow light, fearless
as bit by bit each one of
the crowd drifts into heat
and you are at moments
seeing double from awful music
The morale is an ear, and
under a doorway it is not
necessarily unmoved by the flooding
hiss, or the loneliness of barelegged
women decked by the squall

Mightn't our imitation of a squall
change each other's dignity?
As if we appear prematurely barelegged
and the sun instead favors the trees
who respond with their green flooding
which threatens death to thought
A gregarious tease it is not
You smoke separately against walls
barring air to the ear, and

the fool least of all is fearless
when rage is moved to music
which chooses soloists, each one of
different scornful abstract moments
as lyric time gains body heat

Venus

for Jim Brodey

Awake, compassionate as only
a neurasthenic errant can be
I refresh at the inertia of world

at the retard, ice-chunked river
against which I scrupulously prepare
this duel that rivals photograph

Only the interrogative better matches
universals to formlessness than
the sword tipped with evening's planet

displayed for the banquet and funeral:
Hallelujah! and the color
banana of melted hope!

The wall curves like flesh
and foreseeable habitudes
overlooks, how farewells are lit . . .

if one builds, with vivid sacrifice
bodies up into the skyline
he tastes all the licks and traces

all the dog-peed trails on gutters
through the pantheon *cum* lavatory
in which one's voice makes requiem

Passive Aspic

Fine, fine, the ball plays you, and all an instinct for loyalty gets you is deprived of a country to call after yourself. The cool road and your bare feet soothe what the savagery pulls through the storm sewer, you cast an eye and then a hand, but your blow lands too lightly; come back in truer fettle, you should *sneak* back from the crusher. But O seldom does the song rip me senses through the bullet hole, this ancient jacket from the Meuse, does the song separate the blackened rose from the overall palette and rend upwards correction, excusing division on the grounds of light, its. Through this torn lining you see the black market, you consign yourself to landmarks, and are drawn toward the brittle rusted steps where at the moment of apprehension the sun is focused.

Soften the pillow and spit on the padlock, brush off the hems trailing on sidewalks, and then get a load of yourself, you could just go to sleep in a world without corneal delight, reflections all over the wall as Venus completes her toilet. All too soon the black ambulance covered with ice cream from a collision; too soon the verdict, and the window dressing is torched; soon your relief as the towline seems to draw further into the nautical jumble, where the instantaneous falls over its own fins in haste.

During afternoon the playful demise, blossoms all in bits floating through tangled hair. Hungers whose source is the contemplated empty sky fail the ol' thumper, there is a brief struggle and you fall off the curb, sustaining polyglot hardon. To look at the sky you must be bribed by legs; you curse with your hands full; grinding your teeth drowns out the aphorism emitted continuously by interwoven physical events in sheer air.

Nighttime, mate, and the golden slipper rises in the East. Tankards clang in the stars, the angelus of gamma and beta. The dark praises your own limbs in their feminine aspect, the single candle replaces enthusiasm in the eyes, never moved by desperation again.

Our Lady

for Ted Berrigan

Complete with photomanic *stimmung*
undesired by hatchecks, the obvious
duelist, defiantly without gloves
awaits his hour throughout glib
detailed melon-hues of an evening
when the enemy doesn't satisfy
and vagaries lose loftiness

All of airiness is one room, unerringly still
Desire for an acquaintance increases
with discomfort, and at any torpid
moment you might misjudge the stones
of sweat resting upon blue velvet trance

for striated cleft ore looped deep
with heather, the always effeminate voice
in spite of our manhood
Blame our kisses but not ourselves, afford
us disdain by sheer compass of stride
where dreams and accumulations bed
with flowers that thrive under
insecticide veneers, repelling lunar

gilt—hence the fleecy groves on beamed
torso you hear us mentioning later
when a momentary greatness of description
rewards our straining nerves with
Her atomized refreshments:
a fleeting reverence that bares us
to no one else, her seductive plea
to which, sometimes, we add our names

For You

Asleep in my clogs, after heat drifts
I study light and shadow, I've
become the shadow, when
do I become the light?

And about the hoarseness, it
doesn't increase, but then
I open my mouth, and behind
it there is a flaming fog

To the naked eye there appears
around the fog a glow that drowns
it out, and, after all, the glow
is for you and not for me

Wings

I come off a little bit ventilated
but you must realize the material world
is constantly crumbling under my eyes
it's too much for the novel tongue I speak
the glitter of pavement in my brainstem, you
must accommodate the polytonal grimace
of the set lips becoming a smile, and
you must accept the thin section of arm
advancing across your peripheries to grip you
in pleasure, measuring feeling in your restraint
We have lived through the most furious little
chunk of history for this? that we must
unburden ourselves on night roof air, presuming
the poise and perks of champ pigeon teams
planing the evening winds

until, signaled from the roof with a flag
we become American birds

Eight-Aught

"Tens? You counting by tens?
You want to dance? The music
is way over there through a
crowd, do you believe this is
a gymnasium? O, your dress!
I'm sorry, here let me lift it . . ."

That's one dance I woke up from
where it was New Year's and
the spinning lights had that
nihil circular digit of
Arabian invention, the doughnut
That's what it's like to
sit up in bed with a hardon
from a dream, realizing
with inspired apprehension
that you've been playing
in five decades with the
same old elastic glove

And then you feel you
should wake up, there is
a fight going on at the end
of the bar, I've quieted so

much of my heart in bars
the last decade, as if to
balance the intensities that
radiated throughout, from
shared beds and stubborn assertions

I almost said, "I held
my face into the wind," because
it's always windy outside a bar
The streetlights bend, under
beams as lonely as the
moon's, memories so clear and
inaccurate, I give up what
has been, because of this body
and its implacable need
for a future, in my life it stars
calling another body "home"

De Sica?

They can see it, young
women passing in corridors
—this headache, this heart
and the city to which
it is glued with affliction

do not believe in the
word for purity!

I believe that crimes of
passion tarnish so hotly
little statues are made
of newspapers and lingerie

There is room to be sure
in this world for a soft
lesson in a window a murmur
as you color uncovering
one-footed and
                                    I feel the
weight of desire in my lunch
I am always wanting box
and the skirt falls over my
muttering throes I can only

get it in the gut

                              I rise into

the sky with all the other

people at the end of the

movie a miracle

Astral Roulette

Two quick strides! There!
Bus smokes past my heels, a
slingshot to the Battery, which
is down. I catch my breath
and Sing Wu a song, past those
lights, and their miniature bar
in the window. Ahead of me
in the sky stars are scrambling
from constellation to constellation
shaped as numbers 31 and 9:15
I always believe what's in
the sky at night, O Spanish moon!
And my heart always follows
that brave and unrefined intelligence

from

Where the Weather Suits My Clothes

(Z Press, 1984)

Yankee Green

Frontstage since the age of fourteen. Fine sense of gray was appreciated, but this was dimmed stars calling to the vigorously coerced soul. Instead, he consumed devout wishes. It was inside out, they wouldn't look to his new start. In a quaint deceiving town, plucked by love, inevitably vulnerable. Thus his capacities were marked by an overly figurative sense of death. What was deceitful was saving, when every reply was unutterable, greenery that was just then stepping out of life was put on the door, and removed in smoke from flat areas. Bright rags dying from trees, passions so knowing with utility, a light outer garment to help contain. Flat sky absorbed him with its reach, its crescent deepening blue as the sun honed in on an altering autumn arc. From then on he had a cry in public. It was complicated, this kind of joy. There was no costume for it, but it wore disheveled and felt plain. Vanity cures such contradictions with aggressive environments. One day on an everyday city street it began to hurt. It had been a long time already, and now he was set for life.

Alto

I'm trying to believe this gift is floating on the wind. My ears and nose are open to it, as they are to the reverberating buildings and to the begrimed colors visible through them at night. I walk in solitary motions, and as I pass the meters for longing, their dials go dead as I continue on my way. "That is I," I think, "who am a semitropical mass of longing, who just passed those meters." A recidivist's nonchalance, I am not crazy, I will not protest. But what could I discuss with someone sane? It is all introspection and the discovery of flaws, and I am punishing you because in opening my heart I find myself punishing myself. To me it is a bath that flows off me and out of sight down endless stairs. Yes, you spotted me twice in one night on the fringes. I am comfortable in spite of the challenging sensuality of a young woman's voice that rings in the air there. I wouldn't be surprised if she tolerates me because of my clothing, the ill fit resulting from neglect. Something about her voice damages, a half at a time, the integrity of the material. If I forget about my hair and get a hold on myself, the sky is soon blue and gray, and somewhere there's the day's first brew of antidote. In confirmation thereof, Boreas is the first to blow a horn, and what do I hear but bells.

Corpus Oration

1

Real naive bub. Coming? The court and the waitress and the bliz-
zard that holds them in China. There is no regret for my seed, but
would you please tell the embassy that there's no heir? And then we
walk across a garden of stones, barefoot, regardless of the season.

2

Fun was dizziness before every single chance I took. The dumb had
handles. For heart you looked to your own padded dark, where you
could be alone with a woman without a woman. You came up to the
cool, and like exposing a magician, the little elves and crickets point
out the mechanism.

3

Fate is not always a good soup. Cruelty is not always superficial
enough. The passion is not always timely, to your dismay, in Spring.
Come unto me all ye peccadillos, as ye are the small fish riding the
tongue.

The Eastern Desert

The only place I think there is left to see is Cathay. I just walk, and sit, along its borders with my hat in my hair, and wonder how the Path could ever mean anything to me, of the overloaded flux. It just isn't my kind of cleanup. If it didn't matter ten years ago, it doesn't matter now. It's not B following A; chaos simply reinforces itself because chaos worships remorse. The point is to aestheticize remorse to the point of its oblivion. And you can see how easily this ideal replaces the gladiators.

That noise was only the stars moving. The sweet science of flexibility blurs next to the pole-climbing clematis. The purity of the ditches and the abundance of stones are hell. Resolution takes place at the bottoms. Now that I bend, I lever my blows and glances, everyone comes quickly to grips with an isolated power. You are free to follow the action from the steeps with a certain honor my love of beauty bequeaths.

My Mother, Life

She came as a falling star to the lakes. She the lithesome virgin not to be turned into a tree, she who would never dress like a penguin. An original want-not, she believed in philosophy, but she called it faith. And so her talk entered my lungs and came out as a call to the innumerable vessels that are the wives of time.

Then there is the long span of silence. Every totem to acceptance she wore as an accessory. While the tropic-darkened palm wore its microbe haunt she carried a burdened prose that was barely written, never spoken. She could look and look, and never imagine the stimulation of the lake when she saw the ocean there, so unneighboring. The circle of lake and the core of ocean depicted themselves after every rain, in sunlit rainbow. She had found a complex image that added up. So she rested, and from her rest I derived my strength.

Consider open accidents of flesh, consider perfection of fur in a cat, consider the curatorial mode of an almost wholly passed age, consider the feeling that has a character it emanates from. The fruit is no more costly than its retrieval, the light it gets is subject to cultivation, the dark it needs is infallibly measured, and then there is cool.

Bridge of Sand

for George Schneeman

The sun breaks, red light so fruity to the skin, reawaking from its sea of tearlessness. The softest grit catches in eyelash, melting tissues snag cuffs. I remember not to flinch at my memory, tangential to sleep and the laboratory of stars. The backwards call of the night and its invisible winds had this ambivalent monster and uncouth love. Don't ask me where now they lie, if I offer my ingenuity, isn't that enough in this maze of quartz? That I hold a smoking gun does not indicate panic preceded. So went the night, when there were so many truths to face, so few about myself to turn away. The fogged-in jet's underwater roar, while I rode between cars underground, prosthetic molded to shimmying metal, wearing one of my shoes. Still, I could move in the pleasingly frictive air.

It is me walking that cranks open the sky. Lubricity's luminescence gone, at no loss to Variety's, rising. There should be singers, "We are not all vultures here." Every glaring feature cloned of the finch's song, and the lips of the curb, which never close, refrain.

They are not really singing, those you talk to in Heaven. It must be after the street is cleaned and a dog points a white muzzle into cracks. So lonely as a dog never knows, everything else habitually smelling new but not like the bounty today wants to requisition. I was mistaken, but is that for love to say? Did you ask her? I like my legs, that's all, they are more part of the real stuff they touch. I hang out by these out-of-place trees because at nine morning starts graying, olive skin quotes a poor-girl blouse, and O! poignant feces!

Reveille

Under mercury light the little pup strives. A sinister shadow ducks under the curb—I must describe it all over again, it confuses acquiescence into fertility. How it speeds up the sky and prolongs the night. It is false. It is brilliance in miniature and alludes to her face.

Miles of cruciform sidewalk. Enticed by magazines that are really radios, odd couples nag each other as one strays to a window and one to a cellar. They are expansive because they are small. A tall boy is the man, a short woman is the girl, alarm and its buffer. Both need more than enthusiasm. How mental is your queen when disturbance is the rule! A thousand such couples wave in inert profusion at one figure across the street. I imagine their kiss, I project passion into strange fittings to make it confess a hymn that is my song after all.

I simmer in the half-light of a stoop, raising beers under a pompadour on the first brisk night, pressure more potent than any barometer can read. To see your hand to the tramp of feet is a way to measure strangers. To feel your hair on my finger accidentally is common sense, a way of leading you to me as the watch moves. We return to our bed through the bakery smells of daybreak, sky palling, empty of jets. The schedule is suspended, then resumes like gray dead hands in the east, and I want you never to die.

Look, You

Look, you and I both know you want to sell me on an illusion that is a trajectory. A small but visible object just flat-out zinging, you say, straight at me. Now, I should hate to seem credulous, but I undergo a sick rush of comprehension: this small red casing has been rounded into near symmetry by the air that has put itself into its path, I can only guess at what speed. As upon any such realization, I feel for my lifelike material self as a honey blonde does against sunshine—overwhelming protectiveness. Instinct and experience for once reach a consensus. I said, moving rather quickly by now, forbid there should be a leaden poll where I ejaculate in front of morbid legions. I hold that very curb over there in such familiarity it rises in my grip like a foot of lead cloud, I am one tough tyke. In fact, I make other children realize as soon as possible that the furtive and the infernal are not their own invention. They must refine them, like me, until the uncomfortable suit and the inappropriate drug create a ringing sound, and their ears irreversibly drone of ye tragic flesh. That is all. You still remain their parents.

I've always liked the results, a child on a street, or looking at one out of a window. Children as pigeons. I would like to emphasize the eyes of a child when sunlight is visible inside them. They are fire without smoke, and the heat lasts and lasts.

I'm partly responsible for this. You ever notice how that look of hers makes you feel incapable of defending her? She's looking bullets.

It's pure fate. She may never in eighty years think of it this way, but what she does is adjust the barrel, or cannon, or dart gun, whatever it is I can never see and which aims at me. How many times do I have to tell myself never to look at her so long? Give her a slippery once-over, I should be forewarned, that business in her eyes is one of the magnificent things that is not for me.

The assassin, however, knows a little more than I do. I have the same number of fingers as him, but I think he has more bodies. There are times when I am a regular hero, and I tabulate his duplicity. More often I challenge something random which is not him. It's maybe the wrong time for trying. When I ride the subways a lot I rely on effort, but luck is earned by the kind. The fugitive kind, I mean. Pick one. My heart is with her every time she lifts a phone, and her elbow rises to the V in the sweater she wears.

Lachrymal Humidities

in memory of Ted Berrigan

Lose a brother? Lose a pa? At the sound of the tone it will be exactly sayonara. Meet me in the lobby of Casa Purgatoria when it's Turkish bath hour. We will sweat out whatever the fuck it is that's unclean and inside us, at least inside me. Round and brown and getting cool. Vestigial feeling in the monkey I cut off myself. Having stood beside the catafalque to nominate him for heroism I did not expect a nomination for tragedy to be so rapidly forthcoming. You saw as well as I did how the hot afternoon was grateful to him for bequeathing himself to its mysterious finitude. Dry and bright and breezy and the hours were honey. The shadow of a fully leafed-out tree over our white knuckles. I would have liked to have been holding beads to show how humble and elated I felt. I talked of farce as if it were life. Life itself seemed more than ever high hips in a form-fitting sheath. I can be restfully subdued by the sight of long undulant fingers, please let me show you my entire body! Every time you see me recall my neck sinews, my piano-string forearm tendons, my pneumatic sexual flesh, and my mild and erotic eyeballs—forget the shyness about me that you can't understand. You can easily read in my eyes how voluntary my fantasies are, and how flattering they are to you. Body. B-o-d-y. Ah, the bruises. Later for laying flowers, says the body. O body, O tough stuff, O body capable of sleep. I break the shaft of my spear over my knee and kiss a patch of concrete. Then from hands and knees I rise to my full height.

So Let's Look at It Another Way

Any woman who can give birth to God deserves, I think, a pretty lively dole, provided by God, however, not by me. I've got my own eggs to hatch, and my own coat to button in the particulate wind. Gather around me, streetcorners, and I will give you the avenue of your dreams! I will give three sharp coughs while your fingertips read that spot inside my hip, my pelvis tone, my sixth-story bone. I'll be here when the whole *world* shakes, I'll be compatible to cheapness and to achievement. I'll have ambitions on my mind and panties on my floor. I'll have tons of red paint on my black-paint door. And you know what else? I'll call it "killer monkey doing all this stuff too close to prayer."

So let's look at it another way. It's 9 a.m. and I'm walking west from my door. The only person on the shadowed side of the street, and the shadow is cool, is a thin girl with long wavy hair, hiding her face, which she holds down. White girl slinking where to the east? All night long turned to misery crystals by the Hopperesque walls. I beg your pardon, lady, on behalf of your trade. I see on you the marks your monkeys made.

Invisible monkeys blow into the naked eye, and dust big as rocks. October is taking place so beautifully, and when I sleep pain touches my hair. That's why I always seem to be running past parked cars, and past you whom I love. In some crazy way I am running for your pleasure, out of all the pleasures I could imagine.

Where the Weather Suits My Clothes

Positively on my own again, heart broken so long ago I hardly notice. Romance? Totally gone out of the shaving mirror. The tricky part is when I am first willing to try better nausea. You call that sex? Here I am, longing for you, and you telling me I'm getting what I deserve. Other than feeling rejected and useless, I feel like it's the perfect day to play my street number in the triple. So I meet somebody for a drink in the Shadow of Death. They don't call it "hockey" in this bar, they call it "honkey." Uh-oh. You take the guy on the left, I'll take the guy on the right. Hey. HEY! Where you going?

So there's a hole tonight in daddy's heart where the vinegar goes, and the salt of my eyes meets the soft-shelled crab. My heart burdens the wind. Easy on the Mahler, I tell myself, or you'll wear out the tire pump. The only way I can fall asleep is to imagine that I've been too gallant towards you, and my witnesses are not exactly a bunch of car thieves. Bells and resurrection and Easter Eve mass— now ... you ... want me? Maybe I'm the only one listening to the bell that hears appeals. Its appellate jurisdiction is everywhere. It redistributes the shit even as it flies. Shit and wine and empty shrouds, how much longer can the woody part of the vine hold on? It's, like, cheating the wind of my times.

from

Midnight on Your Left

(The Figures, 1988)

Patria

I am in the Big House outside
Across from me a commode
Radiating from my skull
as from Miss Liberty's—
long thick pointed shafts

Wherever I stand still
the sidewalk first melts
Slabs of tarpaper rain
from the rooftop
out of yesteryear
The past caused it all
to be of America

Give me your runaways
your felon priests
and your mothers
who spit at their own peril
I will hold up this light
fed by their pluck and fight
I will hum through my cigarette
the anthem they compose

In Front of a Large Number of People

Up my backside a core of charcoal does its slither. I have completed my feast and broke all the glasses. Asteroids of smell crash fearlessly around me, it brings out the soldier in my evil turned-away back.

Despite all my efforts life is if anything bigger than ever. At every stage of its termination. Identify the flower inside the flower using what little knowledge I have of women. To think I have become a naturalist!

I didn't say I would, I said I wish I could sing to you. But mercy isn't my song, nor is it in the birds' employ when they wet their eggs. My address is the month. Out of all the lines at least two are parallel after all so they tend to fix me. My calls have graduated from prayers so that the continuum begins to emerge from the downtown background. My eyes are just as heavy as the light. It is not impossible to accept your fingers across my cheek.

It must be ecstasy to die in action. To think children are afforded this privilege. The sky suddenly comes up real close and your body is on its own in the middle of the whole world. Deboned legs of such a drug are roasting in a room next to the one I am in. Hunters are waiting to be paid. Without the moon things go better. All the heroes come out of the firmament smelling blood.

Fur

Something happens
       when you put it on
Blue lips
       Blue Cross
Great tall pillar
       where cat types
go to die fat
       Sullen your forebears
and your half-slip's
       night blue remorse

That's your comet
       sparkles with debris
It can't keep
       me company
And you say
       I'm burning
You suspect lust
       and also hatred
and aye what
       a world it is

I Don't Believe in Miracles

Hard case falls in the shower, slides around the tub twice and the spray keeps on beaming him down. These are very expensive towels here in the penthouse and out front there is I think it's a parapet? The bugler in racing silks leans his head over and hears the bodies blowing around, wind like a dying breath with its hood full of low underlighted clouds. I am holding your air of seduction in the stem of a glass. The bones glow in your face and I become aggressive. I once violated the Mann Act in these shorts for a box lined with that day's furs. My ticket in here is the circumstance of wet boredom. Enormous sopping curtains hang still in the blasty summit. I must get you up that chimney with me somehow. Humiliation may or may not increase my interest. It's also boring to look out windows that are above everything else. I'm like from Mars with the sound off. The whole night is out there waiting to get in our way. First we must retrieve my zipper from the flowerpot by the door.

The problem with when these pursuits suddenly take a solitary turn is what about my dirty mind? Looking around holds it in abeyance and I'm feeling oddly like one of the many faces waiting around the corner. The air before daybreak, it's like something that grows in the sun on rivers. The street sign melts in the spotlight from a roof. And there is that wind again with the bodies in it.

Late Show

The problem is not that there is such dispute, it's that there is so much passion, and this in a town designed for one not to be paid while he waits. There is a hostility towards waiting here, and with it there mount the passions of those who wait, without pay. One who waits is different from a lover, because a lover comes to love the way he must wait. But one who waits is similar to a lover, because the waiting of the lover becomes for him the perfect passion, perhaps more perfect than its reward. By this alone you'd have to call this a Three-Star town.

But not Four. The waiting of the lover, you see, causes him to anticipate surprises, because there is so much surprise in each encounter, because of the city. Of course he is always disappointed, and only after a period of waiting will passion return. Maybe he waits until the first gray, having resisted a dark empty bed. When he walks out for coffee he will pass through the waiting barrier, and the entire avenue will resound with inaudible perfection.

But wait, and diminish grief. Wait, but do not dream. Across the window-lighted sky, charcoal swirls of grit affect each waiting breath. Wait with your hair untended.

Midnight On Your Left

Guy on the air rassles through two choruses of "Misty" and someday I will be with you and lonely too, we have that much in common. No one's going to mistake where we are for the Vieux Carré no matter how tiny the trumpet or how big the sound. It doesn't happen to Frank, Curtis, or Bones, it happens to me. To me 99½ is a lot. Ask any ghost; not saints, ghosts.

Beset on West New York the sun dayglos. Open the mind and catch a chill, April Young, prime de couchant. First one in bed to you, unless you a member of the Orquesta Joven. Let us make merry like the impregnated germs, I never said a good time was healthy. Witness the simultaneous dark event against which everything from the face to the beat-up fender gains a rich disappearing, uh, ness. A miracle by which divas rise from the ashes of visibility. Still want nothing less than a 100?

Now I am the same distance away from you as the hero is from his footlocker. I haven't mentioned you since oranges came out of the pipes and the door barely closed in time. In this race I wake up runny as blood pudding. The smell of roses pouring off the roofs and the scarlet iridescence coats the vagrants. Attentive stillness at 11:43 when dopefiends walk their dogs. The Angelic Choir, that was Warner Brothers, no? I want every scrap of evidence. Can I explain how the dirt rubs off on me and I feel cleansed? Why ask.

Bells toll the long count, cat heat whines in the shiny black underpass. It's a hard pillow as you dream the outdoors and I dream the outside. Candlelight of mirrors sets fire to our letters, and to the sweaters they are sewn on to. Smoke cloaks over our sleeping meat. We smell it when we dress and while we are gone it leaves no trace, like odorless sleep, like numb fingers, and intimacy dies.

Family Jewels

All the replicas soldered with gems
Motors of the ear called names
Your car hydroplanes
    on wheels of vichy

Now eyes are dripping
    The why-for is
    sadly impalpable
I am at the end of the line
    that receives the sun

I wait by a groaning avenue
Traffic invades the crosswalk
I think of children in their spacesuits

Meanwhile the moon confirms
    my incompleteness
I bring to my lips a two-fingered
    hand
A puff is all I can hold

Savory Arrivals

Who would know better than me:
there's no such thing as good taste
Lassie lies beside Proust's sofa
while in his next, Robert de Niro
is Guillaume Apollinaire
Can Bobby get inside our man?
Every so often Kostrowitsky
becomes "Kostro" but most
often he is "Apollonian air"
He comes out of nowhere
while just today
with one effrontatious stroke
Brodey picks up the lyre

You could say I am walking
Walking is my true vocation
I pass hundreds of churches a day
and because for me to be alive
is to talk in one way or another
my feet are writing step by step
the words, they are the tax
I pay to the place called "Nowhere"
I pack in all the news they need

I tell them what a joke it is
to be a guy out here
and then about a woman's hair
in New York's casual wind

Peon #117

A dry empty world invokes
premature withdrawal penalties
I am worthless I am
unoriginal
       I am
religious in my blood-
saturated tie
           O neck
         O gateway
Wrap the ever-growing rose
in Brooklyn daybreak
till I empty my pants
Nobody with naked legs
could ever be guilty
of anything
          like going over
          the *crépuscule*
          du rush hour
and my skin thin as a crepe
stings as lights go out
I hide behind my feelings, see?
My sensations are legless
in Calcutta

The tremor
The compulsive wilt
I am thinking
of Jesus
of getting really high
and of other forms of flight

Johnny Nash, Meet Johnny "G"

Midnight flooze flush full of cripes. My curve went south on me, my back went arch, my feet one-two one-two. Fungus pain white hairs on my chin, finger-like tree-tips in the dark I look in. I wouldn't zackly say I can see clearly now. Ditto the pain is gone. Night is still more than just one half a day, streetlights so many music notations, the golden chord. The perfect singer turns the corner towards me like a bouncer up the middle onto an outfield of concrete. The wall of glare whales where moonlight coats the school windows. The breath without alcohol over wasted street-life jaycees, puff waists and slits for eyes. Time has come to brush off the sheets and watch the glow of dying on the wall. It used to be a cross. It used to be a bridge with froze iron rails. It used to be golden and now it's dark blue. Alert the man in position to score, this once was mine.

Bloody Dewlaps

Everything in the world urges the snow to sparkle where it fell. Hard frozen hickory tree lets out a deep animal grunt during hibernation. Albert Collins singing about recharging his battery in a Chicago blizzard, guitar going "Gr-rr-rr-rr" as his battery grinds. No, my blue ain't zackly Chicago blue. When I think of it, constantly, my blue is exile. Ondawa hills suck down the sun, southerly and fast. In a cabin in January and beyond fever, I'm not the only body in this room. It's the absent manner this other body has that's unsettling. Settling is not of foreseeable stuff, but on pain one can rely. This indicates the break in my heart is a spiral. I have entered a falling heart zone, I take my eye off the road. If I'm going to continue so delightfully I think I will at least build some fire, the trigger is ten degrees.

Smoke is evidence of a life behind me, rising, whipped now to the North by wind, then nothing. Back at the chimbly, however, it streams out. For a certain amount of time. She was like that, deep, and the deeper I went the more muscle it took to haul up the bucket. It tasted so good from her. With every flap of my heart. Oh well, such is life? Say that around me sometime when I've got pluck. She's a draped flag inside of railings. Sure, I'll stand behind that flag, but that don't mean I ain't scared enough to freeze. The bloody dewlaps of the universe dogs break through the basket willows, soundless in the powdery, how do you say, *neige*? I stare at the leader of the pack to let him know that I don't mind dying but won't this time, thank you. What gives with this universe anyway?

For now I call softly from down here. It seems pointless unless what I represent is vitality. The darkest blue endlessly folded into the sky by the personal night, in the absence of an impersonal god. There are heights to rise to. I mean everything's *up there* again. I try not to trail too much mucilage on the porch. I watch a dusting of snow begin in the dusk, white, composed of all colors. With this touch I join all the other slain. It's our kind of longing that allows us to sit virtually in the fire without any more pain than otherwise. There is something special to us about the beds we sleep in. We press our heads to sacks of down that were born not made, and we eat what you eat abandoned on a raft, and the air moving so much faster than me is the touch of this death, the kind sculpted face of death. Touch me with the glove on its hand.

Jaywalk

Lose sundown
    Critters stride
When they glow
    it's burden

The tip of the
    broken wing
is my eyebrow
    wind's my lash

Half a moon
    Stray dogs
Chains no chains
    Little stairs

Endlessly

for Judy Gallion

The stars are so close together I get to hating them after a while. This is all-new territory to me and it's staked out by sets of couples. Nifty, my ass. Companions everywhere just sucks out my coughs. What good does it do you when harm is hovering to know how many names are shared around you? But it is a kindness. Destiny as still life, pain in the most significant face, the whole universe holding you under water. Among the effects, I can't tell your set of keys from mine. And worse, down is up is nothing compared to down is down. History stops in one one-hundredth of a second and I wait a lifetime to see if it ever starts again. My whole life passes in front of her eyes then, and in it a night so appropriate she never exchanges it for daylight again.

Passing slow beyond belief. In ruin I say, sue me scumbag. I say some dream of Satan blew down that highway night caving in her brows with speeding cruel shit of steelworks torpedoing any beauty any innocence at all. I am a fighting beast all wet with combat soup. Broken hands is all that's wrong with me besides my attitude. There's no who in particular fucked with my baby and took her to downtown Mirage. Dripping all around me are tastes of the lake where swimmers reject god and their bodies never drag. Dear body that empties so much, like some kind of bounty pouring out of her. But then these eyes have stared into pussy that is as good as dead and danced on the light in eyes that *are*, dead that is. Tears wring out of sad motets in my head inside the fire. And frankly I am blind. If there were anywhere you could go. Dear head, it would just be losing you. Limits tight around me in the battle between restless air and black ribbons. Stolen like some common treasure.

Pact

If you are out in the rain
If you are blocks away
when animals hurt you

If you are asleep and
convinced you run
extremely fast from roof to roof

If before you wake up
parts of your actual life
seem better than your dream

If you die in front of
the guys who embarrass you
with unpleasant syrups

If you kill someone long after
you were prepared to and for
hours pretend to want freedom

If you need my looks
If you say what burns brightly
If you always hate patience

In the Chamber

Bungle is the password
A slight matter of a deposit
secures you the night's
blank face on the large
crude banknote
I offer all the grease
that's ever been on my
palm as advice:
Don't breathe in
the lights of evening
Moonshine hits the can
bounces off and
consumes the drapes
I'm talking about *here*
where we meet at
the emergency water supply
One man and one
woman gets you
one of each
and some shadows
A caress in the breeze
A caress please so much?
You can't even die without
touching, you can't

sweeten the fat street
of faces
          without touch
I don't retain the melody
that set me, dressed
as I am, in motion
in marriage with myself
It ain't no honeymoon
to take off my breast
and play it
So it happens you
notice me in my
canary shorts and
my crimson fez
Twunk twunkity twunk
My thumb piano, my
very open eyes

The City Keeps

Frosted moths dance over your sights
Your cycle is interrupted on "AIM"
For the third time in ten minutes
you cross corners past an old
Latino, toothless porkpie, fists full
of his own pants, thoughtful
He stares at a short-haired
sturdy tan stray, of proud
saintly restraint in relations
with the domestic class of dog
How self-reliant, what inconsolable
carriage, safe only alone!

Do not be so moved by everything
that belongs to the city
Glazed brown-sugar wheel troughs
Zhivago ice desert street light
but not quite a night for
burglars to call in sick
Not a night for discontent to
surge in heavy boots of principle
Hands are not clasped in power-chain
of mutiny, the sun will
only bring ripening, towards

ego-damage on some clawed doorstep
The creeping lying reflexes stretch
cheap pants, dented empty pillow
stains, strange remorse in light-
impairing clouds, there'll be enough
bleakness for everyone, for zealous
missionary lovers standing-in as
bartenders and bargirls, night throwbacks
Do not be so moved by everything

that clings to the city for its shape
in preternatural drag, narcotic
morning liquidity scare forgotten
as the showgirl, seventy bucks richer by
evening, floats out of The Frisco
coin-op clit spread booth tease
ringing her high and wet, fantasy
transformed into equally useless chains
clinking through dense rooms, drowning
out anxious shouting childbirth's hours
when cold new light carries the tattle
when the name mentioned ricochets and
rises to heaven from the walls of
the prison, illumined by window visages

Steer clear, O victims, for rubbing fingers on
my teeth are the least bit of mud and

a roasted, frazzled corsage from the coast
There'll always be someone else slicker
among vagary lumpen metallic waltzes
They all motor talent sparring whole platoons
in music truce stemmed from manifold
least-elastic *lux*, they on top of it alright
Do not be so moved by their fanfare
so close to the bottom of the city!

It is my luxury to recognize their painlessness
to associate their unpleasant lusts with
preservative acid fruits, delayers of decay
I suck in their souls in order to say
they belong here, all velvety with suspiration
and I esteem their resistance, sunless
and the glowing concaves of the city pour
desolated accretions born of shrill fists

from

Push the Mule

(The Figures, 2001)

The Ticket

Hold the mirror upside down, what you get's World Type B. All the worried fronds shake the same way off the humbled trees I park by. At some point under the scaffold, hangs over the sidewalk, about halfway to the portals of Mary Help, the rent cloth laps damp against my glasses. It's not just in my figments I hear that lonesome coal whistle blow, it's time for it, it's still out there on tracks buried under asphalt on Avenue C. The train can't be stopped, in fact blue twists of fate take their comfort from that woo-woo up and down the solemn morn. There's thousands of us find our hands with our chins and loosen our sadness to the tune. The beast of light's on the far side of four-five doors wracked up every whichway across the geodesic fumes. My friend, have you ever dreamt tears to cremate by? After life, all the contemptible soils to be plumbed-under brown my cuffs, depending on how close I stand. The dead, they bask off singing in time to melodic ways. The leftbehinds tuck theirselves into beds redder than eyes. In their dreams there's stained smocks on the baby, on the cops, on the guys rolling the juice of the hops off trucks in kegs. As for me, I done bent my fallow all out of shape 'til it beguiles the fourth dimension with pollen. Sunday morning, the first three things you got to check off are jackpot, mind, or death. A woman wakes up across town—she can't move, but she's woke up, that's the ticket. Check off the smells, the shit smell, the mold smell, the leather smell, same as in some nearly-November thicket 'midst a vacant lot. Do not, I repeat, do not saddle-up the hound. Seek out the *charanga* violin, 's'not hard to find. Where the world's all stuck-out with nails, move on, adapt. Somewhat. The stops are from rags to rags to dust. The nether is there, so look at it straight on, it's not even most of the story. There's still loins to slap, or hump, or flog, if that's your style. Peace is not in the air, it's but a moment caught on a hangnail. The quick want this from me. They don't want the real flat me, they want my pose. They don't want my promise, they want me ripe. They're fraught all asunder, and I smell of heat from their last smoke, and grease from their last meal.

The Dream You Threw

The wall that whole part of town piles up behind and overflows is waiting to be lanced. Food saved for children on windowsills is only to ensure their hair conceals the way their necks just aren't made for the kissing the backs of. Metal doors up and down every hallway open and close and the air moves this undecided in-and-out way; no one goes through the door; no one is seen "on the side of the door where you ain't"; a harvest of kinds. It's hard to believe how many tables maim children in the smaller rooms. A sheet that sometime served as a movie screen in a storefront church, and now dangles by a casement window, comes loose and flutters over the lower appendages of a brown-skinned doll with yellow hair. Some kind of fluid on the inside of the windowglass begins to boil despite its being a winter night. From way up here you can see the crack that runs across the lobby of the next building over, where most of those who jump land. I can't help there is frost on the shoulders of my cheap leather jacket when what matters is she unbuttons, she's got some high kind of color on the sides of her head where there isn't any hair. The children who follow me with their eyes on my way into the valley don't resemble her at all, maybe not the way I see. She is not helpless, strictly from memory. Itsy-bitsy christmas tree lights, about a hundred of them, are hooked up to the elevator ceiling and they spell out a very particular threat. For instance, the spider might be too small or too brown. She might decide to ask for something warm and wild that very likely a thousand guys are out with flashlights looking for in the most dangerous parks in the city. I'd be inclined to come back with some warm residues of the right food for the right beast. I put a finger covered by an old leather glove in one of my ears so I can tune the noise to the background, which is a dull sound you get from cursing and TVs. I take her arm on a floor we are about to pass and get her off the elevator and down the hall to the window I hear a tall tree scratching, with a branch that doesn't appear to attach to any tree at all when you open the window and pull on the naked tip. This is a lousy height to stand around grieving that kid. The whole hallway is ready to start rising, like an elevator under leaves. I look at her face and the way she scowls at the dimly burning sweet potatoes in the garbage outside doors. I watch her shiver and sweat at the same time. This time it's like the elevator is hoisted by a not inconsiderable moth. The moth shits with the effort and entire blankets covered with stinking filaments land wadded-up where we avoid them. The moth gets smaller, the elevator slows down, and a leaf does a kind of rotary flutter from the moth's butt and follows us out the door on the twentieth floor. Columns of smoke are visible out her windows in the dark room she unlocks. Tufts of cotton cover the walls like hair on an African man's chest in the glow coming through windows from the city downtown. A little girl wearing a snowsuit is curled up on the rug. The cat awake beside her holds up its head and neck unsteadily and then slumps abruptly sideways. I follow her to another room very fast because the tightly packed cinders underfoot are damp and even the most relaxed motion of my legs results in speed.

At the Level of Heart

Riverview skin folds into variants of risk. Silhouette of telephone hangs against early sundown and a guy thinks to himself, "Answer it, man." Song issues from wide-open bar doors where one man's nuts are another man's flux, and it's quaint stuff to shank frank odds. 'S'night before I know it and the only sound of kissing is wheels gluing the last red light to the, take it on faith, sky. Is this the same faith I bereave is so full of cracks, gutless bones leak dust all over my handiwipes? Where's that goddamn phone shadow now I got a real question to quest? The option seduces me, to stand in front of a drawing that is one line tracing endlessly while it shortens up an equal length at the other end. I must decide to call this an arbitrary fruit of time, or to call it a lie. Add hair that was washed last night, and the way it falls, to life I want to give to another, which is a naive, and generous, and villainous wish. All around me I see people bear a visible wrong in a moment of need, and it becomes like port wine at the collar line, lower if a woman is given to holding the chill at the level of her heart. I quietly fill her shadow. I know the kind of longing without territory that keeps random stone under a steady stream of honey, beyond three dimensions. Usually it is in gardens that I fall out of her shadow and land up not in her, but *her*. It is so profound an experience it is measured in minutes. I pose on the scaffold, and it makes sense there is no ultimate face reflected off the hood of the car. What it is is that through her I become folk. Some guys might take the sharpest knife they have and wave it to stand the test of thin air. What I do is hold a beaded-up drop of blood on the whetted side as token of how shrunk redemption is. Flesh hangs above my free hand and waits for the rest of the collage to be thawed. The regular-seeming movement of the sun and the diurnal discomforts of people using tall flights of stairs, that there should be danger in order for lassitude to be valued. A woman with nerve enough to stand up and disabuse me of these exaggerations says, "Fuck these environs, if that is what it takes to fly too high for the hunters, too high for me to lean back in and succumb to dreams." It is only freed of dreams that amazement begins. Ends as a spark between words I use to describe how I want her to go and return, in that order. Then again, someone, a stranger, can see that we are two humans and not one anything else. I apologize if this fucks up the grandeur. The tempo is more important than the elapsed time. The colors inside your body and on it, the wavelengths bombing the street and sending sheets of brilliance up past car windows, all of this is kind of overwhelming. The filament glows, extended from the beginning of my life to its end. The tropical choir fits right in. The color of her mucosa seems like a haywire tint of her outside shades, and I lie here looking for the cue. All I know is, the part of her arm that lay against her belly for a while is the shelf I want to recline on. I lean into the door, shutting it against the last symbol and the last aggressive fool. I am like a vandal slowly stripped of his solitude, waking up to resentment in the act of listening carefully. Luxury is a jungle full of smells that are divvied up, and she has her own. Not to struggle is how to supply wisdom to loss. It waits in a confused rainbow at the very finish. The way she replaces the who who was me is a revelation. I toss and turn on this piece of beautiful wood. When I close my eyes for relief I have to say, "There it is."

Waited For

Assume its mantle and find doom too quiet. Wait for the water to reach body temp like everything else in sight. So, experience is the wine of summer grown from something unlikely, ugly, and, in spring, faraway. Beware that which has sparkle, for its awful dreg salts the mind and bosom with imbalance. Like where in a short season of windiness a male kite is steered into a colorful aperture of a female kite by males only. In reality, nothing flies, nothing submits her memory. I have waited and waited for this bitter crisis and now I am undressed. The train is crowded and when I debark I have my hopes up high. I never fail to cover an obstacle with some kind of bodily fluid. I always think that discretion is what causes my soul to dry and burn. I wake up and the sun and the day that goes with it scoop me clean out. History to everyone I know is so terrible it is in good standing. I love and fail with all my means. Hail the saboteur at the steering wheel. May the people who sit around interpreting disaster go blind. I treat scrutiny like I would flies. A quarrel of scrutinies. There may not be a higher being but I concede there is likely a wizard. The closest there is to equilibrium is equinox. The beauty of your skin and the flight from emptiness you contain elicit compassion. I mean, there are thrones and heavenly bodies and entire conceptions the past would sterilize you with, and flames without smoke that glow from your eyes.

Manger Lined with Fur

Gold stuff falls off the sky and weighs the boxcar down real slow on its rails. Arm takes my hand and strokes the infant so he can't see the spike cocked through the rail tie on his side of the wheel. Steam engine toss its heat in the air, and the babe bounces on cinders where the train gets built car by car. Whistle howls to comfort wee tears, grown special for it in orphanages. Breed them for how little speech in a bloodline voice they need to hear before they'll go to sleep in the darkness of their usual hour. A boy praying for his own lost cause shudders off the point of greatest impact. A pie cools at the window on the other side of where the dog stares over streaked fangs. Boy moves on, flower pressed between palms of his hands. Looks through doorway at the clean blouse on a hanger, imagines the scent of it at day's end. Like his heart's a manger lined with fur. I offer this on the chance the girl will know he has come, for her to make him a youth. Darling, pay no attention to the warning on his sack. He's not the only burglar with royal sword sticking out of a deck of cards. In the darkened room he spreads out the cloth and invokes his métier for her to drown in. The burden of it fills her lungs with honey. An emotion falls like a fish in the desert. He tells everybody that if they crawl low under the firearm they might suck off outer space. This vision comes to him in the glare on oiled wood while those around him sate themselves during the requiem. Sure, he was liable to devotion, but his hunger was for contact. It's some kind of midnight he pegs his breakout on, when courage moves back and forth from her flesh to his. His wonderment collapses the wind and folds it to make public its tiniest, most helpless form. Trees hang still while a high-pitched wail escapes the creases. A nail ripped out of a boxcar wall bends over the new creature's short arm. Steam wets soot to make the signature on the baby's brow indelible. Far off in jungles health roots in holes the baby's foot punches in fruit. The man can't stand there in the middle of deadly smoke and be a boy along with this kid. His own foot bleeds in his boot. What can possibly assuage his restlessness? The blood coming out of one side of the rock, and the water out of the other, is more important than any subtlety. The cold wait at the sidewalk end of the stairs and the moans of the crowd are the entire future of pain. He comes along with the ratty cloth bag in his hand and she knows the mirage is over. The gold dust on the leaf rubs off as it falls inside her clothes, and that night is the zero he will measure from.

Kinds of Smoke

Sun slides down an opaque horizon, drags across the switch, and turns off the omen. Hairs favor points east as breeze packs a chill through this alley. My hopeless neighbors are falling behind on their myth. They unflaggingly mate, if that's worthy of amnesty. Beyond the comforts they provide themselves there is nothing but thin air. The dust of a thousand cars eternally feeds their plants. I refuse to tell you their ailments, they resound off sheetrock and find an open window like canaries. I return from exile in a cloud of dust. I order a beam of light that shines through sapphire to glow on a face framed by the white of one pillow. Where there is a frowzy shroud folded and stashed in a peripheral haunt. After long tramping, a dwelling astonishes me. The face overwhelms me so much it becomes my habit to start small fires. There are many kinds of smoke, but only a few inspire me to ponder the last body not yet removed back to Earth. I come here to learn better how you swallow up what source of light. We pass a storm sewer steam escapes from like there's breathing going on down there. The feeling isn't twisted, it's tangled. There is always this future in which you are yielding. The sides of your body swell and subside. The muscles in your neck go slack, and I wait for you below your sleep.

In Her Own Hand

In a city where poets dine on bitter smoke, rivers taste of graves. A tall slim person names the skeleton of a mood, an impression heavy with bleach and the smell of modern parchment. She gets used to the thinness of the air and the heat that circles the lonely peak like a ring, or noose, discarded by heaven. A poet had better respond with stealth to some appetites. I forbid you to conceal winged creatures in unlit boxes. If you batter black air above your pillow, you could be fated to travel endlessly on a very fast train. Music from a hideout could entice you to spend more than the fortune you started out with. You might blindly inherit perceptions at the behest of a graceless, clean angel. Lift the corner of a grave you honor and search there for a tooth that fits your rations like a key. Every drop of your blood has its source in vapor the river shares with a housekeeping spirit in the cemetery. Stay close to graves where blood is still confined because of foreign origins. Consider those earthy ghosts to be partners in sensation, not thought. Accept, like them, liberties. The dim rays radiating into the night sky from high windows are the perverse weapons of faith and its shadows. Words in your own hand beggar ransom. Congregations of the dead are able to look on you from the outskirts. They nibble on light from no certain part of the city, for something eloquent to come. You're someone who will always slouch opposite to whatever is opposite a full moon over the city. Mist comes close to clear shapes on the surface of your eye. A secret and pulsating place inside you. Smears of different colors overlap on surfaces of your body. You emit particles of praise, and they redound to wrap you in acceleration and need.

Grasp Is Provide

Blurred retention is not to deny how tutelary is risk. Lesson One is the mammal search the eyes do toward some abdominal washboard way up top the diving platform, the one with "His" on the ladder door maybe. Maybe "Whores." Light up the damn'ble opposition of the thumb and the seed, 'cuz there's a leak in the dark where germination flows out of secret conduits. The head of a dick supporting lavish bungalow summons up the paradise a guy never gets off the dance floor. Long colored rolls of paper link reports of mouth planted on ulcered he-butt to gray verbless solitude lost in needle deeps, shut of pain in the family of dope, or spavined by visceral nerve cravings in crack fuck montage. Gravity holds a vessel low to scoop men's drainage in its careless arc, so the woman don't even have the choice to know, the thick red cross over like some dooming angel routed past her bedding. Same starlights flame down hysterical hallways. Maybe I'm crazy but I can see death create its endless dimensions out of wasting. I can see its attractively soiled jeans. Nits of pure gold decorate its hair. Its thresholds take all of my stride to sidle up to, and my forehead sports some beads, nerves racing and all, I mean this gate is more exclusive to pass than any heaven. Meatless hands caress hairless places and make allowances with unrequited mercy. Babe roots out the tit where fights the poison because, well, infants gamble their way onto the wheel, like us. Let clean soft white things surround the state they are in, all who quiver in their cells. Everybody takes somebody else with them, like a magic gun with a longlasting fleshtone shot thrown blind through a one-way mirror. Are you now, or have you ever been, nailed for blissful release? (It's the murk, not the customers, that answers.) The breath fades but still can reach my ear. Deep in the eye a speck twists fine gradations of fear that waits hot and shrewd for the last lastfulness. Ship rolls on fungal drool through the fever night. Algae caps the fitful brow under demented sun. For every cry and oath there are reasons. To the living there is something seductive about control such as sucks these husks. It's time to slough the shames their cookers and spikes and glory hole hikes have wedded to namelessness. Thinking is not grief enough. My hand ungloved under a stiffened neck don't make me a sap. The degree of future shrinks inside the crystal the woman looks into, and she fends off the last ones she wants not to know about the dying whites of her blood. Her double leaves a stain between her legs. Ain't no blackened hand holds no scythe in reciprocation for how she exalts this disease with every fugged inspiration. Over there see her orphan prostrate. Hear her in song call this withering "The Top." Find her head hung deep into the large crude rifled bore sighted on her, hammer high. Crosshairs lavish on the bearer smokeless absolution, and her drying up drags a tore-down sibilance in tow. To do this too well calls for a special bed. Out of his own diminishment, might the backroom guy share with her some quiet sprung by those who war haplessness? The message fails the weight of trust such love needs. A cough is not music one repeats. The man and the woman and the child wait out the debate that goes on above their hair between what their bodies have lost and the powerfulness of their minds to be resentful. What gave a purpose to names cannot float with such a list to port. The breech widens in the channel to keep them in drifting fuels. They find their own handles to grip, and truth is too cruel to inform them of delusion. There is something greater than life in their fears. The option emerges and lasts forever in the air that leaves the room of their death to mingle in all warm cavities, and in all worn prayers.

The James Brother

for Brodey, dead

Fog glows from a headphone shorted and out. Of all the sounds I thought would fall, quiet horn's got the right heat. Slam another beast into the stars. I knew I could achieve blinding gas if I felt deep hair on the man's back. The constant music fixed him even where he was no more. Then the fog went ash gray and stone silent. Smoke fell in treacling streams from tolling bells. What specks of bone outlast sand in lisping Marin breeze? Flag draws away from his family crest, corks pop from guns baying salute. Soldiery known only to those who dream on three sides, in and out and the other one. Warrior mistaken by dogs for a lifer, by sentries for AWOL silhouette on the lam. Some wise-ass guy boring with gifts, they said; pop 'im upside the head so genteel-like, was the way to have done with him. The other side was where stood them who got fascinated with the disturbance and the lurid or graceful or sheerly lost sequelae of fearlessness, of blownout thoughtlessness, of hallowed tongue, of fear. In the wake of exhaustion he got no sleep. He was built without time and no amount of backward looking could possess him of when. Where and who were within reach, how was a sometime acquired taste, and other times the false ringing in his veins took away all sympathy. There stood the bastard king confronting wintry institutions. Queen hid the shave in her lullaby, and the hair never came back. But let's go back to what was made. What was had to be. He took his constitution and elevated it toward the sun and ripped out heart. After that he had this halfway lookout for sanctuary. Man, did that ever screw him up with chance. A trillion grains would have to fall for him to heed, and all the dust that ever fucked with his sinus thing blanched the tree-lined road to the beach. Alone, but for injury. He gave a look head to foot and thought maybe that empty cleft was his fit. He kept alive by never reading "Occupado" off any foreheads, he tried to make up for his push-in crimes. I knew the guy could hear. What the freak was he listening to, though? Maybe some kind of moth hum about a crack torch nebula. Maybe some kind of fuzztone dick, which is sometimes only a dick. I mean, this guy could take illuminati on a pain binge, so they and you and I shed him like pouring fried oil off the parapet, and him, the best defense is relentless offense, crying his skin bye-bye. He got kneed. He got labile off fingernail chaw. He say piracy and you say love, or was it the other way 'round, you say repudiation and he say "What more you got?" He fancied meat of dragon swans, as if the gods were always on his lips. You know how wet they look from the foam and underground soak. I will raise this pitcher to the skeleton man in case he needs to look upon the light through waters. A longing comes over me to tell the abodes of my heart the great nerve sharp has eloped from exile. Despondent scoundrels everywhere sling forth ornaments for his head. He allied with stance breaks and proved to be of use to those so equipped. Without question he was a being struggling in the net, drowning in a dry mouth, weakened by exile unto blathering purity. He lied. A man does not lie when he is mistaken. You want proof? What he was was what he dreamed of capturing, and who could be his witnesses better than the damaged, not the damned? Noisy verbal suck completes his toilet in the dumping sunlight, in the devil's spouts zenning the surf. His power cordons off the frazzled myelin drain in pacific highs. The panic dies with him on wronged hilltops of the Bay. The sky that crowded him and dulled his complaints falls on a dust-brown bed before dark, where his ventricles drew the red mix out of his hapless vanity in extraordinary exaltations. His stygian thing was sleepless shivering to know. That pain sprang on moons and led his arguments to expensive resolve. Handicapped god almost lost on men and femmes. He told with his name a telling weird, and romance drunk with tomorrow's smoking riffs on some unsophisticated finger chart of his only device. He was that fucking pure.

Pouring Gulf

It's the road behind lets my star off the hook. Up there in the night sky, it's part of a slipper designed in tiny white dots. From this curb I watch a woman in the back of a cab tuck her furry wrap around her neck. They call it a gulf, and it's pouring, man, it's pouring right now between us. What can you tell a guy who missed the chance to wire his mandolin, once the century starts to fall under the weight of its own sparks? Time has this shadow, and once I'm in that shadow, the shadow can't be said to have failed, right? I muscle in on a wall of snow that's the road ahead, pretending to breathe. A young woman plowing through the cold keeps pace with me, breathing even less. The only thing that can break my courage is memory. The tension in my hamstring is automatic, it teaches not to stop when full. Young woman in ticket line puts her cheek against the back of her partner's shoulder is a symptom. The passage across his face of a warm mask peeling off is the gulf again. I might as well read a bone in her face, or a line in his palm, forget about my star. Disappointment replaces the strong with strength itself, every man-jack gets to be a wife this way. There's always a glow in the sky to implore, as if it were lying ahead instead of there, forever in the past. I'd lose anything, as long as lassitude falls away with it. Let's see how long you'll stay with me before I start staying with you. Farewell, though, is such comprehensive music I sometimes forget it takes humanity. Snow going dirty fast is one measure, like a bar written down off an aircheck. The young woman lifts her cheek away, a hooded look over her eyes,

124

a wave of some cello vibrates in a faraway of her own. Then she visibly adjusts to the tone like a stone to runoff. A piece of wood in her secret drawer patinaed with lacrimae. Every sound she makes has more vigor than his. The way ahead of her is white, and all around her intense color. Loss is so becoming to youth, buried as it is, in gain. And how beautiful a disguise is summer.

To Keep Saliva Warm

The wind and the presentiment in the same dark minute, and I hobble to an even bolder place. Certain effects of your flesh catch a fiery remnant of day to one side of the unlit room. Reflections from street and sky and airshaft range across scraps of music lost onto the table from pockets. I close my eyes and try to imagine what the exclusion of your voice would do to me. Reassure me that rainwater runs off your body into my glass, and your sounds run over my throat like a bandage applied with pressure. I come to, a little embarrassed by the nothing smell in the room. Energy closes in with suggestions of wilderness. The sound of one antler falling through the skin of the season's first ice. The world and I are obligated to keep saliva warm in young mouths. Pain causes those lips to twist awry from parching, or from bloodless insult. I escape as best I can, not knowing will they follow. In the dark here, many a hand can wipe swaths of malice. It's all coming down around me and I can feel it happening, just like a king with scars. Pain with its intricate beauty, and pleasure with its willingness to sacrifice the present for the present, queue at the aperture. Music chooses to make imminent the communion of a man with the other man he is. I do what I can with this limitation, all the time thinking of the safety of those young mouths. The number of sensations I carry at any moment is pretty amazing, and the fruits are knowledge and liability. Look at this: I'm sitting here in the dark, and along comes music to perform a maneuver on my body from the side and from behind. Nothing I do can stop this from happening, which makes it an elevation of place. My eyes glaze with incoming things. A light grows from under my feet, and anchors and ripens them. It steadily moves upward and violates me with time and decisions. What I took for a maze is a perilous and necessary sleep, on pillows and rags, of the young. The dark melts into the passage of sound, be it of breath, or of blood, or of bargaining prayer. Please leave me the hopes of a demon. Young mouths swallow in sleep and do not know the existence of fools.

Unless You Tarry

Reach over the wall of cabs to turn back dust. As long as clouds lit from below loom close, it's a cinch to share one's least breath. Young woman with rare skin hears distant music, to and fro she goes from the corner with hip to the one with hop. Buried under oranges where I buy my ciggies there's a snare drum disappears by day. By night it's smokeless fire through one end of the scope. It don't mean a thing unless you tarry with small cries come out your mouth to tell you've been trapped. By light of bottles lost in the cooler, read your rights off the cuff on her left wrist. There may be nothing else in her to cherish. Hard to guess where she really festers, not so where she sleeps. Maybe she can help me suffocate after all. I can't stand to breathe anything but unstable gas. Anon my tastes moisten-up slake by slake. I wallow faster now through hood ornaments either side like salutes of swords after a soldier weds and his bride like a white widow shines on his dress-blue arm. All the love and combat in the world should yield a little to spare moments such as clown around on this dog-beshit pave called 12th. My muse, the one tuned-in to the faraway freeze-brained raga, she disembodies next to an intrepid Ford and re-ups her flesh passing a Nova, ten steps behind me at 9. I can actually *hear* her be fickle in the eponymous meantime. When she is close and weird, like now, I never cease to be disappointed that *al fresco* doesn't mean nude. I got plenty muscle and it fêtes my thought. I got a grip can condemn rough paper to creases darkened with oils. For the last hundred steps I have been singing, and the odor out of my mouth stands free of its broken mold. Steam rooms full of dead poets shape their coteries after definitions on my flank. They are vexed I walk on unendingly. And in their hot wet room they celebrate the rubbish I spew through the sieve of my lyre. I disturb them out of love and low dirtball bedding. The very thought of them and my spit together make wondrous terrible paste. Collar up and wind crawling my back, I scan for two-three panes of glass that don't reflect anything at all, and, sure enough, they beckon.

from

Private
Lemonade

(Adventures in Poetry, 2003)

Everything Beautiful

Buick, big old boat, purrs
Backs into the square of moonlight
where the path is worn

Notice you must the pang
in the air
       You hear
a little of bells, a little of hypnosis

I have traced all this to my body
Everything beautiful, and everything
that ever goes wrong

One giant light of green
and one of gold, inject the glow
chosen sky by the city

Shadow Feet

Sweetheart   debt   blue heels
The dominant hand
of my partner
            at 4 o'clock
on the power steering

The little bit of time
you have, knowing

I had better wait here
for the canned laugh
Shadows joined at
the feet
            smoothly
smoothly tread

Disbelief

Usage
        clouded and fast
                Gyrotropic

Eye out for
        her
                least
                        expression
Hissing of leaves

As words go
        meditation
                is small
She apprehends

This window
        for diminuendo
                forecast

She looks abstractedly
        at the fender
                pull away

Private Lemonade

Some days I forget
      In my own home
            high stakes charades

And spouts pour copiously
      on every sensorium
            to flood the hobo camp

He answered to Friar
      Himself a wandering few steps
            in two trips around the basement

Melody is more than a name
      An obbligato in front of the stride
            I saw him peel his own ivories

It goes in one ear and stays put
      This exacting moment
            Undetectable difference

That Place Anymore

To be learned
          from but not
                    to believe

Influence
          surroundings
                    demonically

Even your
          sarcasm shows
                    you loyal

Twelve strings
          Sympathetic
                    yellow jello

Your hand brush
          ashes from
                    my eyebrows

That is just
          horrible
                    Have a seat

Rockin'

Blue wrapped in gray
Leaves underfoot orange
Intensely sweet mold
A gift

It should be one of us
Source of meager light
Just because I move
        Autumn winter autumn
        Frame and shoot

Weeping too unusual
Fatigue an indication
        Change unnoticed

Check for bruises
Say open your eyes
Squalid but fruitful
        Cease to exist

Rockin' back and forth

Bleach

This winterless Spring
Equinoctial bleach in highlights
In thrall occurs a lapse

Your voice over traffic
Never less symphonic
Waited and waited

Print of rattan on your calf
Succinct and nearly cruel
Turns lamplight lavender

I am gone
You are gone
Let it now begin

Anywhere

Foolish bright nowhere thing
        Hand open through bars
                Wind rattles over crap

Penlight searches for map
        There is one token left
                Dull crease of moonlight

Conservation of error
        Brokenhearted boy you hated
                Dry sheet too a mistake

A girl can stand like that
        Lights on wheels strobe
                Palms drip on shoes

Downy Skin

Compared to
my life
my life
is long

Accomplish
a tenuous
fixation
Memory

Anything
anyone
can, will, or fails
to intimate

It is older
I knew it
long ago
Her downy skin

The Beautiful One

Like a flower bending
from momentum of light
      Anotherness
Placid as a lead snake

Knowing from inside out
Cause, in effect, a search
      I love you like
the mountain loves sand

Spread ground on the hand
Dawn and day slightly coincide
      Remember me
Force you to listen

Front Seat

Seventy-eight ripples
      Forty-five shakes
Light warped on dull
      uniform Ike eros
No need to worry
      The man don't love you
An item of undercloth
      The uninterrupted front seat
Everybody singing
      Merry Christmas and inside
It seems one hundred
      years of Christmas war
And if I want to
      love that woman
Always end on a chord
      Suffer in vain

Knowhow

Never quite habiliments
See-through trees
Eyes floored by leaves

Your name comes back
Everything heated
Dress for the cold

No one forgets
Assemblage aflame
in store windows

A very long letter
First time time succeeded
So many bus rides

High degree farewell
Later much later
What not to feel

Pool Cake

When she sleeps on the floor
When the umbrella blows
into her hand

The whole landslide is missing
She treats me like a conversion
I am a probability

Eclipses her in sheets of snow
How many emotions on
the tines of a fork

Her particular disguise for dust
The haves are equidistant in time
You could say everything is minus that

To those who waken stealthily
Sew up the hat real neat
Frost ascends the blade

It

You you you *what*?
How you do without?

Curves end in curves
Not me she's after

Shed without walls
Eventually femme loses

And it is so small
Change

Can't Say

Can't say I don't
        Fire hazard or mouthwash
                Mud on the gizmo

Grimy handed
        Baby dimples
                Hair like breeze

Terrified
        Object was never
                before without say

World sways around
        Other farce renews
                Short bridge to sell

Protection

When I go
        out I don't
                fall asleep

Children will
        be always
                on target

Cold bites deep
        into mixed
                company

Houses fall
        that have once
                already

Protection
        remains how
                unlikely

I am glad
        You begin
                to worry

You'll survive
      You'll forget
            Shiftless luck

Dim, Dud

Dim realism, dud parquetry
pried off sidewalk
Commonality in due course

A hand no longer cold
Illusory violet branch tip
The girl looks ever younger

Vitiated serene kids
Reflections off my reflections
The scale played this evening

Trousers cling by down draft
Directions balance at zero
My own resonant footsteps

Every day begins the same
I sleep whenever possible
Large indifferent appetite

Weathered ill-cared-for hands
I am tired yet ready
The helpless reappear

Dream Marble

Midnight shines like sun
Her language rhymes laugh with cough
Her continent produces "shooting fog"
I witness a dead planet glow
through a glassless window
in the elevator

Pockets develop among hills and bays
where the world is small and
always smells the same as
her home
        I go to it
but in fact it is here
I have always had here with me here
My first impression was of
dream marble statues and led
me to perceive that this city

in honorable, selfish ways
emits into the air I breathe
the power and felicity of pronouns

Flakes

Muddy plastic spoon
Barefoot on colas
First they nab the tramp

Words sort and sink
Ash glitters on her collar
Jumpseat vapor smell

She interrupts herself
I too blow smoke
Can't hardly overhear

Farewells then walk alone
Night briefly unwraps
Inevitable hallways

Food of Others

Consideration
      for my sleep
            Bird of night

And by day
      getting used to
            the food of others

To be consistent
      with unkempt hair
            Fluff on fingertips

Your cheek is cool
      Your core is hot
            Song of your weight

Parade

Inadvertent jitters
Everyone knows this street
Point of view all over again

Hat on it
Clipped heels bobbed tail
Then you know real rancor

Ghost in mother's milk
Heal worry heal weakness
Find private ocean

Voice loud love strange

Slope

I cannot say
       handbag for you
              Armrest's so cold

I do say it was
       all in weak minds
              Highway post mortem

On the drums I
       might black out
              The sleep of your foot

is vortex and yourself
       is wanton goof
              Where is everything

Known to you

Whole

I am lost and distracted
You have all the right ideas
I try to be whole

Abandonment
Stench eyesore
Whose bidding

You relative
I correlative
Debris all kinds

Be there sanctions
bearer wizens
Play by head

Back comes first
The moment comes forth
Handling of water

Bereftness once sweet
Singly together past
that beauty occasion

See you some
Albatross sensations
More always more

Heavy Building

Heavy as a doll
Prove to me I
have come full oval
The red phone I
answer it's
mongrels left to
pick up rocks

Left foot more sure
I don't notice
the cigarette until
my fingers are afire
The lighted arms
The mellowing time
The vanishing building
I swear it was there
and I once entered

Overlooked Nomads

Complaint set to
music, chantoozie
stands on my feet

Overlooked when
leaving, full glass
drains into air

You are one clue
when you are your own
The wires burn up

Remain away
You nearly die
day after day

greater than I

Wavy

Boogaloo
the best you can-can
Time hangs in braids

There is room for
that hip in the
blazing gold drum

Do not hasten
The crosswalk aglow
Maybe learn nothing

Signature footsteps
I know what to do
with the wrong dream

from

City of
Corners

(Wave Books, 2008)

Waiting There

And you go down that street
Rainbows ahead bling you
like midnight never does
and I wonder where
evening will be tonight
My loved ones waiting there

I pretend my swagger
through debris
is the holy dance
of the many my days
On the remotest sidewalk
facing the moon
I cannot say
the orphan still lives
and you recognize
the battleground
You can hide her in
quadrangle dirt
The buildings are
old and half blind

With an enemy
like daylight who needs
the psychology dime
Hips do the work
and I cross the world

Comes with Galore

Dabs of light on the pocket
Oblivion is always legal
Hey, you know, there
are sweet accidents and
hair with unearthly sheen
Stand aside for the keel of litter

There never were any heroic marbles
They stifle everything that hard
Even stone rings of fragility
It is plenty they attend to
and the perversion of taste
that comes with galore

Mercurial responses then splat
Brilliance at a mere simmer
while she considers her odds
As chance has it they are infinite
She sees herself scurry and hide
She claps an eye before white lines
and lives on up close
to where the beautiful king

All the Hair

Snow weeps jewels on trash
Can't sleep nights in that dream
You approach as arpeggio

Murder arouses ministrations
But I have reverent lips
Always you follow a form of child

You and less than you
All the hair is the question
More time than I figure

I hope only a little bit
I had better not help you
Smoke rolls down the street

It makes no mind if it's real
It is I who begs to differ
You are only mostly you

Starling

Leaves the car wash
No no no no
She wins that round
Reservations procured
Soap suds on open shoe
Like a starling in sunlight

Essence applied to neck
Don't wait for modifications
No lipstick on filter
Blonde to detonate delicacy
Slide off the stool just so
Playacting out of fairness

Contributions unenumerated
Purse always in hand
Plate glass mirror by streetlight
Person intent to be in place
Dialogue not yet occurred to her
Now the stage is upset

Follow equals wander
Perhaps her empty secret

I'm no good at others' integrity
She seems to wait for me
Left no other choice
We cross with the light

Convenience

Come out now they are gone
One engine I think leaves twice
Somebody must be the other

So calm so aware
Unity is entire, you detect
a convenience where you'd expect

No less than one can be
a witness in doorway
Punch to arm along directly

All because I want her any cost
Dissemble and negotiate
Curve rolls over body

Require breath in identical ways
Diverge because it is hip
Do not save changes

Beat It

Something happens alright
Anatomical luxury
My body your body tattoos
Rafaelo aka Ralphie says
nobody knows but Lupe
Gets you a sixth-floor window

So alive I forget to beat it
I turn longing into admiration
I could sleep in a curbside
excavation but I don't want to
There is no more meaning in
the responses of others

I point out to you
that I breathe
Instructions always incomplete
Give me that mood crap
And this will always haunt you

Silhouette

Weary excuse for doom
Sparkle on oiled brown forehead
Rising sun bustles from girl to girl
Spills tones of luck on lack
Lonely woman theme gone solo
Mad skimpy and tight's a sight
Untimely floss on appointment day
with a bow to the night from a runaway
Verizon relay on a belt
in touch with obstacle number one
Variations on implore and spite
Looks alone make a man dizzy
Elaborate a history of affection
drawn from kitchen living bed and death room
Hope out on bail for all my effort
My relations are dying, got that under my feet
Dreams go on living beyond my means
I can't understand how discipline
is of any concern to the annihilated
Depends on what she considers survival
as she dodges calamity
Silhouette her hard face on the wall

Straining to Hear

You so livingly glance
Dirt again yields bud
Satisfy me that you
have salami grease chin
The sun pretends to pull
more than just so
I enter the penetrating sight

Brevity affects the skin
Wherever I sleep foam pillows
Blackout windows night before
Crumbs, sugar grains, comedy
Sun's retreat to window box
Can't remember love in May
Nipple hardens in twilight chill

Sleep larger than life
Softness is not meant for you
Hair blown forward then back
Straining to hear over car radio
The smallest unit of knowledge
Aftertaste of rosewater
Weight of the world in my mouth
Sidewalk rises to meet her feet

Floss at the Barbecue

You walk toward me
No you don't
Had me fooled
Standard deviation to elevate
lingerie to beachwear
Chemise to uncompromising
floss at the barbecue
Cheek not smooth and
your dark presentation
Speaks first words softly
Well-understood coyness
for her to be
living on high
Bewildered, distract myself
Don't expect that heavy voice
At the sound a few
shift in their chairs
Spoons rock against crockery
She repeats herself
I follow her to the limits
of my eyes
Subject to evacuations
I imagine details of

light housekeeping
What are her shows
How often she balls
What she is so used to
it is truth

Loops

Burden of cloud so calm
Mess completely exculpatory
Maybe you prefer dry twenties

How does Saturday go
Smoke loops over keyboard
Restless, ignore brilliance

The regal flows of it
The microtones
The furry parts of it

Everyone else leaves
I need you again
Loudness of your heels

Nearly Perfect

Barbarities abound
in sanctified drag
Liquidates the nutrients
Let us dine afloat
past the nearly perfect skin
of I forget her name
You don't have to whistle
The door of cards (the house of)
swings face up against
the wall of numbers
I walk through with you
over scattered kings and queens
Bury them with extreme prejudice

Some peace in the uprising
is not necessarily sound
I want one abuse at a time
dissected over and over
to the rim of equity

I learn the cares of a hairdresser
I see her leave extensions intact
The influence of bangs on
again, nearly perfect skin

Proximal arm is not for her support
The shame that never wants
maybe not in her deep self

Cold moves me on
I expel a moment
of smoke

Newcomers

Out of nowhere wind chimes
Imagine layered cloth napkins
Sleep's garbled translation
            Sinister bonhomie
            of paradise
About all you can
expect of newcomers

Wants you to stick
to your current line
            Wants you
to suck out all the air
from the Sterling Street stop
Notes passed you by the tiger
Insignificant natural light
rakes the momentarily
            abandoned
            sweatshirt

The One Who Turns

Loss of reflection
To long to return
Trust in companions
and in their idleness
I cannot be one of those
like whom I most feel
Substantial and bleak
in alien fraternity
Kneading the ball
Clasping the necklace
Turning to the one who turns
toward you half asleep
Complete disregard of attachment
to remember all my life

Any Country on Earth

They are crowded and swirling
They are all white and do not
correspond to any country on earth
Don't think that of me
I'm, like, gratitude to trap sets
I'm   Wonder who you with
           On the comeback
           One night at Flora's
           Anybody and me

I must not be listening
At midnight, strangely, visible
I continue to subordinate everything
to the emergence of bite
You know how helpless
           Don't lift that way
           Box of light on the floor
           Come into its shadow

Realm

Not capable to see what will happen
Hosts come and go and you submit
Your past envisioned as wires and rivers
Like everyone else you wear your bloodline
only nothing makes you a darling
Between that and your short fuse
The sinews that convey touch
When the current drains off you
and every cell quivers on its stem
Now you know the spy, you know your value
The most forward parts of you sway
since the twilight they emerge from
is both night's and day's
They compound in irradiated fatigue
You are entitled to derelictions
Accept this condescension as universal
You are in a realm beyond ailments
All the light one can admit
when most visible are the utterly heartless
You are not born able to wheedle
I hope your ankle will be a relic
A floral name such as Lily
No use to pretend the day is maiden
All her senses disguise and quicken
at the feet of her own disciple

Remedy

You remember, we are down below
Very bright, everything vivid
Reward of the sleeper state
I grow without the one who leaves
Evening passes like creation
I look in unlikely places
The other side's behind me
Happens

How many stars per organist
An intruder is compatible
Still in her youth with secrets
Some kind of namelessness
Planets count but only one matters

Remedy the exposed side
Rag doll rolls off pillow
Hips butt and thighs packed tight
Your daughter like a mountain spring
High up above my eyes

Get Help

Land should never slide
Waters dance so massively
There is no respite
Clouds high thick and cold
I inform you, of all people

Still a lot of smoke
Can't say I'm innocent
Get help with the transmission
Meanwhile, how to stay warm
What the neighborhood does

It isn't really haunting
Happens a second time
Perfectly clear face pale
Eye-catching plaid gloves
Apart from the weary

The Signs

Not easy to summarize
Entire summer, in fact
Lovely face, sweat beads

Maybe gifted in crowds
You read all the signs
Stop ten feet short

Check budget for warm affect
Hey you, with the plate
Must seek teen empress transfer

Exposed skin intimate *au deux*
Air dirty and breathable
I wait for your name

One Percent

They think nothing
matters in darkness
Card between fingers
Felt on tables, walls, heads
Stand up carefully
See without looking

You have jangles or not
Engine warms nerves cool
Only one percent truly knows
Naked trees humming wind
Short change embarrasses
I can tell "pregnant with"

All that you're after
Create your own fairest
Deep reservoir flow
Impossible to say
I will never roam far
One need of many to sleep

from

Singles
and Fives

(Fewer & Further Press, 2011)

Your Island

The trance transmits water
from tree to tree
I am afraid to state my love
It is unfounded and
chokes on foliage
I subscribe to your face
I cancel my shadow
A lucky stroke of
burnt umber on cheek
The empires of countless
patrons cut loose from
your island your legs

It darkens on the hour
It is not where you were told
To all appearances
the emptiness at the end
repeats itself
You sit in the lobby
The privacy surprises you
You are partially borne
along on it
This is not when to relax
Suggestions
They go on and on

The room has an illusion
that it is a park
You see labor has made
it natural and healthy
You are where the plot
is already dedicated
There is something
over a park like
the frightening depth
underneath a swimmer at sea

The room is also a harbor
Large things come to rest
Tide is predictable
Fish have their season
in the odor of the partner
And then they assemble
who are always with her

To have a trowel
for an astral woman
To have wet cuffs
The room speaks to
her and I speak
to the roof

Where Else

Dirty low cat momma
Think left go right
Tired of your mess-mess

There are a lot of ingredients
Where else, the world
No monument to nests

Hardly sudden at all
Something better falls asleep
Emerald spoon listens to me

The mess is semiprecious
Odor clings to her blouse
Hold the trumpets

That the origin's irrelevant
Let's stick to the dictum
Surroundings crowded out

Dressing table fission
Ten feet out the door
Utterly stunning

Token Faux

Of all the seasonal tasks
Spring pass swiftly
Never have and never will
Serves up by doffing gray
bark donning mauve
says streetlight in sunset
Refresh her makeup by it
How hide the shiner
in an unseen-gun world
Where you sing and
the cage enlarges
Token faux survivor
Blind beauty of the
criminal-minded girl
Who'd let you go

Where you are missing
all over a small world
Loss of name
Sight unseen

Getting Tough

Halo sits like the
City of False Hope
on the Empire's crown
Rain falls like nails
The baby quiets down
Time to go

Without refuse around
the street looks bony
The second it fleshes out
paper glides and particles
tsk on fenders
What the woman's look says is
don't need nobody else

Which is where I wancha
Tables turn and now I see
the lapse in your imperium
Your children are fat
and they are getting tough
Thought you should know

Can You Tell

Happens this time
in answer to indecency
Lit by the yellow
shop windows cast
Unkind to you, that light
You say, Sit, Ubu, sit, or
Hey, I like your weave

This avenue for instance
Gateway to escapade
You can see from the
beginning to its end
All-embracing greed
Distracting appliqués
of altruism
Small pomme de terre
Can you tell whose
hand on the basinet
and that does what for you

Warmth all in the light
Sight all in
garage park hallway
Morning's dusk on pause

You stand body in profile
What you don't fill
in the doorway stays empty
More than overcome
I know you're there
and unseal my lips

Tell the Angels

Wherever you come from
that's where they are
Get off the table
and adjust your lap
One life can change
your memory of events
Pants into pantoums
Silken skin into marble
Certain things that never
change the other way 'round

Hat in hand
is a far cry
Sidewalks glow
a liquid brown
Spattered hose noted
A lake is the corner
Surface jauntiness
and enterprise traverse
Clues in disarray
Stepping stones a maze
How to tell
a tether from
a tenterhook

I choose to look
up and into
the next face

I can tell the angels
by their tarnish
By their attachment
to brands
Steer angels from
under awnings
weighed on by slush
One for my shoulder

At Second Glance

They are convinced of
what you husband
Animal odor wakes up
Now resolution overheats
barely inside the door
Her scrutiny self-contained
and unaffected
Clasp hands in front
Wait until the handle turns
Which door will that be

The convincing seems
to be over with
Her self-assurance
develops warmth
My palms dry a bit
Small bottle of dude
Stand clear of bright windows
Call it comfort
or confidence
What creates an impression
Soft chesty laugh
empty of coyness
At second glance

the door is a crown
Behind it she
reclines and asks

what I'm used to
All my words float inside
frames on the wall
I raise my hand to see
what is in it
Something I do
not recognize
A swatch of floral silk
It looks good against
the leather sofa when
I toss it there

from

Tiny Gold Dress

(Lunar Chandelier Press, 2012)

Tiny Gold Dress

Days so fleet you have to've
seen unruly ones
I do all the time
Someone I soon trust
puts your hand in mine
Just what I'm looking for
Start with the body
and search me
Won't find me sleeping

I dig my six feet
and you stand there in
your tiny gold dress
Can't believe my eyes
Your smile knows
Your ever-so-slight lisp
Ahead of me in the
opposite direction
Big man alerts me

I shed little bits
of chivalry
I caress like one bereaved
Forethought and hindsight

in the flesh
Peanut shells under bed
Lamp nearby of
fire and roses
Ribbons of smoke sketch
momentarily an orchid

Black Lapel

I touch I stay
The glass empties
You notice so little
Remember later
Moral anergy
This round's on me

Bathed mauve in bathos
Crowd meanders
with a purpose
Disappointment
makes me tipsy
Stars poke out of
infinite black lapel
I return to your eyes
Brows no longer soothe
Delusions enter
discourteously
Ha-ha ha-ha ha ha

Dispelling Face

Mirror boy mirror girl
Never can you tell
in the mirror world
contradiction from ambiguity
Alliteration of tires at noon
Inconsistencies of the equal
and the functions they suggest
Axis pass through one
dispelling face
The prices she pays in life
I watch through the veil
When she's ready you
know there's no replacement
She signs with a snake
three times of her neck
the communal letter of odium

Reverie comes hard
Sometime granma looks good
Voluptitude that never resolves
Seems always snookered
three feet from the well
Back of the hand
large with veins

Eyelid gleams lavender
out of shadow
Sundry things she
wears at her waist
Hip things to do
in captivity

Despite Murder

She deserves better by someone
Desire for the worst to happen
Feel like she really join
communal genius of misery
Resist entering because of the bricks
In this heat you've got a point
Outdoor weather suits your clothes
Streetlights gold against
turquoise horizon after
a mean sun disappears
Bunch of girls mosies off
in search of the offensive

In the day they called me Lucky
Problems were beginning
even as countless others were
not resolved despite murder
She left me uptown and
I came down with my pants
over my head walking backwards
Assured of glory like
her other million fools

To You For By

Somebody somewhere
couldn't say nothing
'til I call myself self
Choice profile in
the crosswalk an
encounter again
with wonder
Something shows
of all that can
contain anger
Just as cocoa
butter wipes off
brown from clean skin
Send for yesterday
yesterday, clock
the race of particles
through the tomb
that surrounds
your marketplace
with hecklers

What you suppose
recklessness calls
to you for by

name in a
private language
It shunts you to
thoughts more precious
than memory
Swipe your card
Descend the steps
and incise the crowd
to undercut this
your epiphany
Subway platform
induce such
civilities as are silent
After the first
hundred there's
nobody else around
Safe now to touch
small faces with oils

The Urge

Miss all the time
Keys of sterling silver
Can't find the door
Anthem ends and you
are singing alone
Lift your cheek from
the metal you tread
Step of a burglar

Street retards ardor
Substitution of
stellar streetlamps
Door gone the way of ice
No way heat doesn't
blast, there could
be smoke any minute

I recall an unusual
way to count her fingers
without using my own
Dark enough under the tree
Silhouettes two into one
Overlapping in arrest
Seen on the move because

the urge to stop is
hosed off this sidewalk

Enlighten the amateur
There's no stopping now
So many buzzers
without names
Doors without
distinguishing marks
Just like they say

On Turbulence

Those who listen
make their way
among your friends
Incomprehension
deploys elbow
to elbow
Railing cools
under my hand
Streetlights
multiply shadows
Preliminary lift
on turbulence
Ever ready to fly
as if high above
wooded hills
A passionate
exchange out
of memory
Uncontainable
synergy
Legs hair face breasts
all overlap
Sweat pools in navel
Air moves again

its observations
concluded
Mercy, mercy
the clouds are bruisers
Nobody knows
Nobody will

Lip Read

Take into consideration
the broken route run by wind
Engage the sidewalk as
dance floor for whom
I ever attend to
I insist to be bidden
The short unfiltered one
notes the call
Progress to decay
through blossoms
She reacts to my appearance
with sympathy
Another verse of
the unrequited

But the light is harsh
Lunch in hand
with shade so spotty
Perfect skin is rare
It arrives a newborn
and departs in family arms
Cheeks of an amphibian
to be shaped by the past

The train I miss
throbs below ground
Footfalls lessen, lip-
read goodbyes
Of all the traffic laws
to observe, cimarron
red car parks in the
pyramidal glow of
navel oranges
The hand that inspects
is not in mine
They call it raincoat
Leg dries matte brown
Press breast against stone
Ditty in a minor key
I hear and am healed

So Real

One of these days
you begin to cherish
the landmark
you see so easily
By the window
memorabilia
The woman the cat
Roil with transience
which incontrovertibly
stagnates, its fossil
the overlapping frets
Ashes cold are shrines
Breathe life into them
Warmth to spare
Offer incense fruits
exquisite pewter
Power, breath, power
All in my dreams
Everything so real
Clothes more colorful
Drinks so cheap

Rain, Boy

When floodlights impair
Ample darkness confound
She has a handle on
public dishabille in
contrast to the blond
decay of leaves
My surrender
is conditional
Zephyr's chilly reprise
Close brush with significance
that beast I
forget the name

Rain, boy, beating
on those windowpanes
Umbrella decked with
skull and bones
Hips in a crouch
Wavelengths across
Stoop light lost
in reflection
Her face completes
an annunciation

Close around
wings beat
Shelter, one supposes
opens out, doors in

Many Duets

Galleries where shots
were silent
Cathedrals of raunch
Stage set with
men's room
How many duets
extinguish on
accumulated air
Forgiveness built
on distrust and
disordered prism
of memories
Countless eggs thrown
out of bepeopled drabness
What looks best
to me blinds you
eminence aside
Read fortune in
handbills as they swirl
There is license in
the color of that lip
of those thighs
All of it on loan
Long as you know
your way around

Correct the Air

There are friendships
that resemble curiosity
There are friendships
that dissemble equality
There are friendships of
no standards at all
Correct the air that
stands here drowned
Kiss of amelioration
undoes a man's esteem
Forget the judgment
implied by rags
hanging from trees
Knowledge isn't
a meaningful word
but as a bubble
it will do

Betrays Nothing

Dignify her comeuppance
with lowered voice
with myth with backbone
Offer semblance of longing
in arbitrary words
Her indolence the dance
of contingencies
She swipes the glass
off the table and
tilts back her head
If the wits about me
are indeed mine

Makeup betrays nothing
Her expression pleasant
but interminably fixed
She is jealous of her voice
It is hard to share
now it is the one she wants
Her grip on the napkin
too tight for drying lips
The same lips part
and I believe her

Who's Left

Doll's in love
Dust everywhere
Guy with a crashbar
Curtains sop a puddle
Chair is gone
Look who's left
So much gets flossy
and ill in the ghetto
You can tell by an odor
A big pipe I mean big
Comforts are invented
No regard for solid colors
Makes you aware
of speculation
Silver where most often
a gene would have indigo
Mismatched cutlery
Flawless blades discarded
Newport filter
after you sit on it
Something almost daylike
Change makes way
for changes

That ring veiny red
all the lightless time
No bones define your hand
It turns away my eyes

from

Gold Stars
Wet Hearts

(Faux Press, 2014)

In Form of Seashell

Railings intersect
to make a V
Clumpy yet dry snow
makes feet musical
Hear her call my name
Reflections of youth
await youth
Pause of thoughtless
consideration, then
in her direction

Moon in the Fish
Yes, like a spoon
To watch her smooth
her skirt with a stroke
A gift for analysis
A gift for coinages
I'm only here to listen

Now back to the movie
Leaderliness
a kind of beauty
Appearance covered
by multifarious light

Doorway in form
of seashell
Pass under leafless
arcade, her
color deepens
The scene dissolves

Snow hardens with
highlights of
cinder and piss
I bow to the static
in your hair
Powers a city
of millions
Of them I am the one
who sees how

Doubles

The neat get mounted
Pasts cross, at first
evasive, then touch
Look down if you still pray
It is music to death's ears
The lot taken away
defined by the victor
When it satisfies it is true
while I'm submerged

The coffee house tips left
when I collapse to the right
The reinvention of something
spit between teeth
when that's forbidden
I find you three times
in the same morning
Those are doubles, sweetie
Your hand trembles slightly
Afraid of bridges
Afraid of silk
Breeze undoes itself
around your ankles

and when the light is beat
down to nothingness you really
do use black paint to describe it
If you press this button
a horn sounds
If you press that one
you don't know what
It gladdens me
to tell you this

Headlight Tag

In shade of headstones
prolonged silence
Myself leaks in

Only two feminine hands
Tattoos the same
spot on each

Heavy linen cloth
Two bars of color
One for neck, one for waist

Words from the heart
The heart must be breaking
One dies of the thought

Getaway on foot
Game of headlight tag
A building waits no longer

Rapport if durable
Desire to be finished
The sorry survivor

A very private talk
It's always 2 a.m.
Can't part, can't stay, good morning

At least to feel your hand
Uncurtained window
Push keys across table

Cool without the mask
A kind of pidgin affection
Time to go meet them

The Title

Volition escorts you midspan
Right wipes off left
The title is yours but
instead you pass me
the album of fires
Miscreant means well
Thunder turns into
the air I breathe

An oil absent of light
Knife on your palette
Forget replication
Maybe your skills
better suit mistakes
They soften hearts
They divide enemies
They promise a context
Excuses happen
all by themselves

On the way is
where you stay
I should throw
the word away

Without time a note
can really last
Fingers arrested
forever on your back
Hollows of darkness
along your arm
Your most flattering light

Gold Stars Wet Hearts

The angels when you get there
cry at the beauty of it
The other side of the curtain
where it's intact, a melodious land
Locusts leave no sky behind the clouds

A body of blue material
We gather in its wake
like a cadre of winners
The sovereign leaves
everything up in the air
Flavored coffee soaks the carpet
He hearkens to a distant diva

Somewhere beyond the portents
My appropriation, please
Realistic toy escape on one hand
Lie mistaken for mine
scrubbed onto bare walls
Foyer dreary except for the portrait
Bodies of water, macerated
feet dry in shade largely
determined by gender

You hear about celestial lowlife

Physical genius *chez soi*

Cards, gentlemen, gold stars wet hearts

Dog on the shelf hungers

Malodorous choir in glitter

The pot grows and grows

Transparent chips reach the chandelier

Chanting now louder and near

Got a Million

Bricks, stains under floors
Shiny fluids in drains
If I could save the street
you propose is there on
A between Undone and Do
What that delivers you
is an appealing disgrace
Exit playing a tune on my teeth
Give way to mahogany mallets

I never see ferals anymore
Whoever it was goes to my head
Three wires, three is all, and
even the magnet's turned off
You already got a million of them

A one-footed dance, call it
a soul because it's stone
There's no jingle to it
Throttled or muffled
Hand so carelessly wounded
Wavy line from north to words
Closing in the fog arouses
my penchants like spring water

Small leaves on floor
curl in the dark
Old balled-up roots
Play a rhapsody on a toy
The rest a dream
where my intended lives

Assemble the Colors

Mouth falls
in my hands
at the sight
My feeling is scent
to the sound
of rotors
Colors at
a dead run
Face after face
and then—
Maybe you've
seen the portrait

Hand disappears last
behind the door
Pink finger pads
drawn back and
the lock tumbles
There's an old
song with rhythm
I need
Stairs all slivers
Fluorescent landings
Fan of shadows

Next flight down
the bulletproof door
Out of it the what-what

Eyes pan the opposite
sidewalk and
assemble the colors
Rays in the air
convince me that
person is not her

A Hundred Feet

With what your mind, loosed
by cyclone, washes the deck
Nothing of filth, insurgent rather
Vessel with an ontological hull
Your navigator is detained
by indiscretions
Her sun-ripened arm
Temperature at which
tears no longer touch
She whispers, when do you leave
About my reply, the languid
and the practical, I walk
on a hundred feet

Anyone else could have
applied the makeup
Under olives still on the tree
An order of time that bears
more conviction than my own
I am used to these stairs
but seldom behind you
Perspiration that doesn't bead
is termed a glow
Without lights is light enough

Steps descend, stairwell abounds
with colors out of your person
Your heels like dancing taps
At the door, a moment of silence

from

Knee-length Black

(Free Poetry: Boise State University, 2014)

After Quiddity

Quiddity after quiddity
assembles, the same window
view without mirage
since after the fire
So studied in character
it counts for minus
Sheltered by nothing
but four windbags

Some of the feet march
Some exercise an upright
rotary motion
to achieve a horizontal zeal
A destination magnified
by fatalistic epithets
Light-metal trophies
worn throughout the ceremony
over highballs because
she is electrifying

To have it innocent
for the act not to be pure
Every abandoned *flûte*
of not-champagne

is to bargain with captivity
To give oneself is to
quit an empty hygiene
The colors I can offer you
to sit on are either
hideous or a godsend
to your pale, pale skin

Red Tide

Compounded of
       public decumbrance and
             heartless mobility
the sky waits for me
       and shows its red tide
All those aweigh on
       a discrepant sea
swell and ebb
       on blue hillsides
from which I spring
       after a whale
Turnover in sky
       Cloud stalls
             and falls
into the glowing
       river of ore

The gummy sod
       of extinction
The return hopeless
       and hoped for
She to me in her sleep
       provisionally to care
she knows not where

Which Next Minute

Glaze of remission
      in daylight
Finely tuned jubilee
      Small tree of
      silk as hat
I find the lever that causes
      one to prowl
Impossible to put off
      morning
Outdoor bed
      where it's always dry
I am at peace
My shirt wilts

Relations feed back
      the hundred watt
bulb in your mind
Suffer the thigh to abide
Sell the clover
With regard to
      things sanitary
wash the baby's ass
with reliquary water
Not bad for
      two days by train

Things different after perjury
Foot traffic a blend of
        vibrations under scalp
Which next minute will unplug it
Wires to ground before quitting

So late so dark it
        doesn't wash
Lightning not likely
        to strike a shadow
For now the body
        it's all inside

Box Set

Pepper on tails
      Talons in silver hair
           The monks fade
I'm not afraid

Constellation: The Chair
      Aurora in box set
           If I were taller
it'd be love straight
      from Atlantic Shelf

Talk to me, ions
      Bonds break atmosphere
           Join seated to standing
Posture produces hair

Which hand should touch it
      A glove drops
           through atrium
Wall-to-wall air

Knee-length Black

1

By morning there's a planet to scope out
after all the mischief and unstoppability
Everyone is perfectly honest

when it comes to swing time
for the condemned, like the old
French joke about
"x is not-x plus x"
The body as wile-sick
and unseen already

I don't notice the dream
despite the giraffe and the gold mine
I don't even notice Alaska

2

Hair like water falling upward
Wet-alloy air's paw on nose
It's not just vicissitude that

makes her wealth glow
Weather is an "it" and
she is a self-limiting "more"
The gift she makes to you
of bathlessness

Of course there's a wrong day
though you can't tell yet
The materials gather in bits
for a story in short features
They will share the first word "When"

3

When grackles last come to Sunnyside
Young sculpted face, "Tiara"
perhaps her name
Knee-length black fiberfill
smells of kitchen
Doesn't cross herself passing churches

In a window looking down who
can treat of her thoughts and
subliminal her to safety?
The flag there is hard to remember

Nights recharge on deep trains
Sunnyside lacks living shadows
to compromise monuments
The living reject statues, names
made of conceptual words
and pricelessness
She trains her eyes on where
invisible voices would be
were they heard

4

Dream ripples as he ties a towel
Doves, mourning and rock, descend
in a bacchanal of snow fuck
The riot is soothingly twee
and full of messenger drums
Daylight blanches, yet fully clothed
The body within infinite reach
Something touches, time and again

Umbrella and Eyes

All's in motion, mostly retreat
like water to leak, like trees
to bird's-egg-green paint
It arrives, rain of misty expectorations
The human voice carries feet, not yards
I pick up my roots and flow

So different in temperament
umbrella and eyes ascend over
rooftops up the dress of sky
It is home in a hotspot, grease
on the side, manifolds of appetite
Further from the skin, great pain

Mandibles sadly responsible
Panache to panache, trees heavy
with sweaters have long residence
and no obligation to shelter
The very young step forward
A retouched sky, ghostly
jurists behind it
Air with grimy disregard
waves hallway to hallway
which is when we meet
down here, where the gods are

Uncollected Poems

Trip Wire

In vain seclude a fossil of dream
a flight of scapulas
Starved and shrinking moon
Where I've been, be gone
What makes it a bigtime crime
to spend the rest of my life
shaking like a lake

I meet you not far from it
Waitresses serve me as I pass
Attractive disputes in their own garden
When the wings open again
and everyone gasps
It spreads like coral or invitations
Trip wire worth more than
that ring on your finger
The world smokes the world
as fast as you master it

It's embarrassing to lay claim
Violins you cannot hear in dreams
A trough in the sand where seas
accumulate when it rains hard
A rim of mountains that

the glacier will move
and then deposit when it
evolves into livable ocean
The dream itself the clue to wakeness
and what it is laid off for

Certainty of the railing
where she parks one hip
No sleep in the etiquette
Stoop as the court of sharpness
in song or in solo
She sits top step and everybody
must turn and face up
The weary stuck onstage
Whoever parts the sea
will tear her dress
It begins with a siren and dissolve

Daybreak is just the ending
Figure reclines near beaming window
Animation within begins to sort
Semblance and the noise it makes abate
Step feels sure in a soundless world
Recognizable at first sight
Colors bright, consequence imposing
Refreshment at stake

One Hand

As if a fatuous explanation
Fifty minutes of moonbeam
Its roaming poison
The smallest corners
of the world
seethe in it
But I generalize
Beneath a faulty streetlight
a dark shadow from bridge
of nose to smooth chin
Are there really but
a thousand names on the moon

As if the moon's inside them
coils of weave high
on her head
with the finial touch
Pinnacles bright in her eyes
Blessed are they of tempered zeal
The tide's power with
no proof on river wall

The half that is illuminated
includes her Sea of Belonging

One hand holds Samsung
touch screen alight
Free hand on dark side
Toe of knee-high boot—
palm-size Milky Way

Evidence

It takes a long time
for me to collect evidence
The woman on the beach
for instance, is right now Uptown
How can a street be
haunted, a city refined
Where it would never occur
to you to retrace your steps

In my dream your eyes
which never move from mine
give you a headache
You wrap your head
with a shawl, Nguni
voices chant fond harmonies

You groom your feathers
as an act of squeamishness
What if you spook at
only intelligible sounds
What if you dance by yourself

I'm ready, have been
The chill is not

all in your mind
Cold falls like dust from
holes in unseen stars
The bridge that looks
like a rainbow to you
is a wet crosswalk
Far behind us now they
discover how little we ate
for how much I paid

Fa-fa-fa

Like the crest in her hair
bully comes over her
Chewed up and out
she shuns tenderly
Spoken in an instant
a speech of the hounded
One arm gilded one chromed
Groomed and accented face
Unfinished eyes where
rudimentary things last

Last one to touch the car
Bag on backseat a mistake
Wherever she is
the center approaches the wall
Headlights blink at 3 p.m.
Now she really moves
Count the accusations
Find out for sure this evening

If you don't know the signs
the empty moon is full
Mad early, loopy late

I could stop the hang of it
but I go on watching
She brushes by
singing fa-fa-fa
for want of words

Load of Ice

Reaching out to sleep
An arc of attention
The wise are usually
not ready and send
trouble for that load of ice
A guy can only wait so long
I say, and go on waiting

Wide-eyed I see her
and lullaby with secrets
She handles bitterness
with gloves on and
lets down her hem
on the fly, I can see
a glittery cheek by
the light of my phone
Joy girls get the left hand
I grab it by the wrist
and slip off the watch
into a pocket of her coat

I can still smell the wires
The vines I sleep on are
alive with fracas

but her sigh's a real sigh
Heart attack flames lick
the behind of my sorrow
I don't even know the time
but she can count in
five languages and I call
that plenty damn fine

Missing Planet

One more link and it rains golf balls
If some thoughts are padded rooms
in a hovel, let this one be a rose
on a bed of chilled noses
The dagger you sharpen after
every use brings on this fuss
Dust sparkles on the dashboard
A certain quadrant of sky turns black
An alternative receptacle for the eye
Something to keep but not in mind

I groan a bit to reach the wall safe
I really can't tell you much on
the subject of paradise but there
are moments when I'm out
on the unicycle and the missing
planet on the crosswalk
is my Fata Morgana
There's an irresolute comfort in
resting my head against
the butt of a lamppost

The mess won't clean up in fire
If you're missing a few bobbins

If you want to repatriate
If you hate the mumbles and hiccoughs
I wonder at this desire for splendor
The look I see is not a backward look

To be expected in a parade
So many faces constitute a quiz
Last word of words is a maybe
I tremble after the defection
I run into the Maypole head-on

When in dreams I misbehave
Window opens on a dazzling space
The opera, at the beginning, is infinite

Index of Titles and First Lines